ROUTLEDGE LIBRARY EDITIONS:
WOMEN AND WORK

Volume 4

# WOMEN, WORK AND FAMILY IN BRITAIN AND GERMANY

# WOMEN, WORK AND FAMILY IN BRITAIN AND GERMANY

Edited by
T. SCARLETT EPSTEIN,
KATE CREHAN,
ANNEMARIE GERZER, and JURGEN SASS

Routledge
Taylor & Francis Group

LONDON AND NEW YORK

First published in 1986 by Croom Helm

This edition first published in 2022
by Routledge
4 Park Square, Milton Park, Abingdon, Oxon OX14 4RN

and by Routledge
605 Third Avenue, New York, NY 10158

*Routledge is an imprint of the Taylor & Francis Group, an informa business*

*British Library Cataloguing in Publication Data*
A catalogue record for this book is available from the British Library

ISBN: 978-1-032-27038-8 (Set)
ISBN: 978-1-032-30506-6 (Volume 4) (hbk)
ISBN: 978-1-032-30511-0 (Volume 4) (pbk)
ISBN: 978-1-003-30547-7 (Volume 4) (ebk)

DOI: 10.4324/9781003305477

**Publisher's Note**
The publisher has gone to great lengths to ensure the quality of this reprint but points out that some imperfections in the original copies may be apparent.

**Disclaimer**
The publisher has made every effort to trace copyright holders and would welcome correspondence from those they have been unable to trace.

# WOMEN, WORK AND FAMILY
## IN BRITAIN AND GERMANY

### A Project of the
### ANGLO-GERMAN FOUNDATION
### FOR THE STUDY OF INDUSTRIAL SOCIETY

### EDITED BY
### T. SCARLETT EPSTEIN, KATE CREHAN,
### ANNEMARIE GERZER AND JURGEN SASS

**CROOM HELM**
London & Sydney

© 1986 The Anglo-German Foundation for the Study of Industrial Society
Croom Helm Ltd, Provident House, Burrell Row,
Beckenham, Kent BR3 1AT

Croom Helm Australia Pty Ltd, Suite 4, 6th Floor,
64-76 Kippax Street, Surry Hills, NSW 2010, Australia

British Library Cataloguing in Publication Data

Women, work and family in Britain and Germany.
   1. Women — Employment — Germany (West)
   I. Epstein, T. Scarlett   II. Anglo-German
   Foundation for the Study of Industrial Society
   331.4'0941   HD6149

   ISBN 0-7099-0976-4
   ISBN 0-7099-0978-0 Pbk

The Anglo-German Foundation for the Study of Industrial Society was
established by an agreement between the British and German governments
after a state visit to Britain by the late President Heinemann, and incorporated
by Royal Charter in 1973. Funds were initially provided by the German
government; since 1979, both governments have been contributing.

The Foundation aims to contribute to the knowledge and understanding of
industrial society in the two countries and to promote contacts between them.
It funds selected research projects and conferences on industrial, economic and
social subjects designed to be of practical use to policymakers.

Printed and bound in Great Britain
by Billing & Sons Limited, Worcester.

# CONTENTS

Contents

LIST OF TABLES

LIST OF CHARTS

## DEDICATION

To all the working women
who perform the balancing act.

## ACKNOWLEDGEMENTS

This report is based on a study of 'Time Management at Work and at Home' conducted jointly by British researchers from the University of Sussex and German researchers from the Deutsches Jugendinstitut Munchen (German Youth Institute, Munich). The bulk of the research expenditure was met by a grant from the Anglo-German Foundation, which we gratefully acknowledge. We are particularly indebted to Ms Barbara Beck, Secretary General, and Dr. Hans Wiener, Projects Director of the Foundation, for their unflagging interest in our studies and the continuous encouragement they have given us.

We were fortunate to find firms where the management and the staff were eager to co-operate and share their experiences with us. We are greatly indebted to the two English retail stores, namely the Peacehaven Superstore of the Brighton Co-operative Society and Roberts Bros (1), as well as the Beck Kaufhaus in Munich, the German department store where we conducted our enquiries. Without the firms' supportive attitude our research would have withered. All our colleagues at the Familie-Arbeitswelt Project Gruppe, Gisela Erler, Ina Fuchs, Monika Jaeckel and Greta Tullman provided invaluable help and support throughout the project. Our thanks are also due to Rosemary A. Watts, who as our Project Co-ordinator tirelessly and efficiently looked after the administrative aspects. We must also thank Michelle R.P. Epstein and Traudi and Alastair Wiggins in Britain for tackling the unenviable task of deciphering our messy manuscript in order to prepare a typescript; and Birgit Braun who carried out a similarly efficient job on the German manuscript. Finally, we gratefully acknowledge the permission given by the Controller of HMSO to reproduce some of the official statistics as corrobo-

# Acknowledgements

rative evidence.

We invited representatives from the different interest groups we encountered in our studies to let us have their opinions and Part III includes papers from several of those involved in our project: one from Dennis Higgs, Personnel Manager of the Brighton Co-operative Society (BCS), and Joy Kuhn, Till Operator at the BCS Peacehaven Superstore, where Kate Crehan conducted her anthropological style study. Angelika Fauth, Personnel Manageress at the Beck Department Store, where the German study was conducted and Margarete Riedel, one of the Beck sales assistants, also wrote contributions. Moreover, there are also accounts of their personal views and experiences by Robert Hammond, USDAW organisor for the Southern Region, and Sheila Morgan, a trade union activist. By inviting these different individuals to voice their own opinions on the topic we have been investigating, we have tried to avoid the gap which so often separates researchers from the subjects of their studies. How far we succeeded in this we let readers judge.

Kate Crehan
T. Scarlett Epstein
Annemarie Gerzer
Jurgen Sass

NOTES

1. This is a pseudonym, because the firm preferred to keep its anonymity.

PART ONE

INTRODUCTION

Chapter 1

TIME MANAGEMENT AT WORK AND AT HOME

T. Scarlett Epstein

At the beginning of this book we want to stress
that we consider its importance lies in the many
questions it raises rather than in the answers it
provides. In preparation for our study of 'Time
Management at Work and at Home', which began in
October 1982 and went on for two years, we conducted a library review of relevant literature. We
found a considerable volume of publications which
discuss the work situation, as well as a lot of
articles and books dealing with various aspects of
family life; particularly in the field of 'women's
studies' there seems now to be a mushrooming literature. However, only very few investigations attempted to examine the interaction and interdependence
between work and family. These two spheres of human
activity were treated as if they operated separately
and independently from each other. Most of the few
studies that link work and family life concentrated
on professional couples (e.g. Rapoport, 1978;
Edgell, 1980). Since professionals are much more
articulate and vocal in making their demands than
are unskilled working people, the focus on middle
class couples is understandable, particularly because they also make good and ready informants. But
it is just as important to discover the problems
facing the large numbers of working class couples.
This is for obvious reasons a more difficult task,
which so far only a few researchers have tried to
tackle (see e.g. Campbell, 1984; Hunt, 1980).
    There is a great need to investigate the over-
lapping relationship that exists between work and
family life, particularly among unskilled women
(Gutek, 1981). With our study we intended to help
fill this glaring gap in available knowledge and
understanding of industrial society. Many more
studies of this kind are needed before we can begin

3

to grasp the total implications of the changes that are taking place.

## WHY WORRY ABOUT TIME MANAGEMENT?

Industrialised countries are presently experiencing a social revolution of tremendous force: long established practices of human relationships both in the productive and domestic sectors are being challenged. The great divide which has been separating the world of work from the familial sphere is beginning to crumble. There have of course always existed strains between work and home. But there has been the implicit assumption that if some adaptation were needed it is the family that must adjust to the demands of the workplace - indeed this has been the case so far.

But things are changing and families are no longer prepared to adapt at all costs to the requirements of the work situation; and consequently the disharmony between work and home arrangements is growing daily.

The traditional division of labour whereby men were the breadwinners and went out to work while women backed them up by staying at home and looking after the family is now being eroded. But though there are beginning to be perceptible changes in the intra-household division of labour they are still only marginal. Gardening, decorating, household repairs and care for the car are still mainly perceived as the man' responsibilities; an increasing number of men with working wives are beginning to take part in childcare and many husbands now wash dishes. Yet the job of managing the household, i.e. planning meals and shopping accordingly etc., besides the numerous and arduous cleaning tasks, still remain predominantly in the female domain.

The increasing numbers of women who join the labour force therefore do so at a high cost to themselves. They virtually take on the 'double day': they have to perform effectively in their jobs to ensure that they will not be dismissed; at the same time they continue to shoulder the responsibilities of running the home and looking after the children. This often puts a heavy burden onto working mothers and makes them prefer to work part-time rather than full-time. In these days of high and still growing unemployment part-timers offer a welcome flexibility to the demand for labour. Therefore, there is a noticeable trend for female part-timers to replace male full-timers, particularly in retail distribution and the rate of female labour force participation is likely to continue to grow. However, working women still predominate only in a limited number of low-skilled and semi-skilled occupations. The same pattern prevails in Great Britain and in the Federal Republic of Germany (see Charts 1.1 and 1.2). 'The range of jobs open to women is very narrow because the labour market is organised in terms of sexual apartheid' (Hunt, 1980:103). In 1971 'all service industries employed over two thirds of all female employees' (DOE, 1974:16). Whenever men and women participate in the same occupation, male hourly earnings are considerably higher than females'. 'Women's weekly earnings expressed as a percentage of men's fell from 55% to 51% between 1950 and 1970 in Great Britain (Davies, 1975:18).

If going out to work involves women in a lot of additional responsibilities with only low financial gains, one cannot help but ask the question why increasing numbers still seek formal employment. A variety of answers have so far been provided to this question: some claim that the broadening economic horizons necessitate households to ensure additional income to meet their rising demands for better homes, cars, holidays and the like (see p.45), others consider that in times of high unemployment women's earnings are essential for the running of the home (Weijman, 1983); while yet others believe that it is the social aspect of work which attracts women to employment. All these arguments which try to explain this complex phenomenon in terms of one determining variable, whatever it may be, are inevitably over-simplistic. There are obviously a number of different influences operating simultaneously on women which account for the growing female labour force participation rates.

Even though increasing numbers of women seek employment, their emphasis on home and family is still apparent. 'There are ... conflicts and contradictions in their self-images. They are splintered images where incompatible ideas are found in uneasy co-existence: for example the belief that men and women should be paid the same money for the same work exists alongside support for the family wage' (Cunnison, 1983:79). One cannot blame these women for being unable to sort out their ideas about the relationship between their work and home situation, when official views still regard these two spheres of life as strictly separate: 'A wide range of social policies, in fields such as income

5

maintenance and services for children and elderly
and handicapped people, continue to be based on an
assumption that the primary role and responsibilities of men should be in the field of paid work,
while women's should be in the home and in the care
of other family members, be they elderly or young,
disabled or able-bodied.... Work and the family also
continue to be seen as totally separate policy
areas, dealt with in isolation by separate departments even though the relationship between the two
areas should be a prime candidate for the joint
approach to social policy urged some years ago by
the Central Policy Review Staff, 1975' (Moss,
1980:13). Official policies thus continue to ignore
the conflicts with which working women have to
grapple.

The trade union movement, too, has not yet
taken on board the problems facing these women.
Women 'do not become so readily involved in trade
unions as men because they perceive their jobs as
being less important than their domestic life which
is the major source of their social identity'
(Cunnison, 1983:79). Yet the percentage of women in
trade unions has risen dramatically. Sydney and
Beatrice Webb estimated that in 1891 less than one
in 200 women manual workers was in a union, compared
to one in five men (Davies, 1975:64). In 1950 16
percent of working women were trade union members;
and this figure had risen to 27 percent by 1975
(Hunt, 1975:8). Though the proportion of female
workers who are unionised is still increasing they
are drastically underrepresented on union national
executive committees. Men still retain control over
the routine running of unions, from branch level
upwards, even in the unions comprised mainly of
women. Yet there are changes: more women emerging
as shop stewards, more activists at the branches
(see pp.192-200), and more women taking their places
as paid officials. Progress is not steady; it may
come ·in sudden onrushes, but mostly it is slow and
halting. One reason lies in the reluctance of women
to come forward, another and possibly more important
one lies in the often unwelcoming response to them
of unions, where male power is entrenched, and where
little attempt is made to accommodate to women's
traditional responsibilities (Cunnison, 1983:77).
For example, at the 1975 TUC out of a total of 1,030
delegates there were only 84 women. Out of the 15
affiliated unions, with more women than men in
membership, five sent delegations to Congress which
did not include a woman (Hunt, 1975:10).

In most industrialised countries the 'Women's
Issue' has become identified with Feminist or
Women's Liberation Movements which tend to be perceived as only concerning themselves with the
interests of middle class women and as remote from
the realities of working class women's lives. Women
in the middle income group, who largely compose the
liberation movement, have choices which working
class women do not have: to work or not to work, the
kind of work, part-time or full-time work, to
further their education and thus upgrade their occupational level and so forth. Most women employed in
blue-collar jobs have no choices - they work because
they feel they must do so. To them many of the
issues so important to the women's liberation movement seem removed and even frivolous compared with
their own bread-and-butter issues (Raphael,
1974:32).
This lack of attention given to the lives of
ordinary working women triggered off the research on
which this book is based. We realise of course that
'time management' is not only a problem for working
women but also for men. However, since men are an
integral part of the established political system
and, therefore, have ample possibilities to form
political pressure groups to represent their specific interests which is not so for women, we focussed
on 'How the Other Half Works'...
We considered it both timely and necessary to
find out how working women perceive their own
problems and what their aspirations are and then to
match these with the relevant views by management
and trade unions. This multi-dimensional aspect
makes this into a novel type of report in which we
include not only the researchers' materials
involving often verbatim interviews and their
analyses, but also contributions from appropriate
management, staff and trade union representatives.
By asking how women cope with being employed while
at the same time still having to look after their
families we tried as much as we could to involve
directly in our studies all those immediately concerned. Each of the different contributors to this
book, however, brought their own particular slant to
the general question of time management and this has
meant, especially in the case of those participants
who were not researchers, that there is a wide
variation in the specific issues they have chosen to
focus on. This diversity is interesting in itself
and says quite a lot about the differences not only
between German and British culture, but also between

the 'cultures' of employees, managers and trade unionists.

## HOW TO STUDY TIME MANAGEMENT

Our study differs from most others of its kind in several ways. It is cross-cultural involving studies of retail stores both in England and West Germany, which should provide some insight into both the regularities as well as culturally-conditioned differences in the context of how female employees manage to meet their work and home requirements. Most other studies that attempt cross-cultural comparisons do so by conducting surveys and/or by using available statistics (e.g. Galenson, 1973). By contrast, our analysis is based mainly on primary data collected by using the participant observation method customary in anthropological style research: we used the work situation rather than residential areas as the point of entry. Kate Crehan, our investigator in England, not only worked in different jobs in the two stores she studied but also resided for a lengthy period with one of her informants from the Brighton Co-operative Superstore at Peacehaven. Our investigator in West Germany, Annemarie Gerzer, also acted as a saleswoman in different departments of the Beck store she studied in Munich - as a married woman with two small children she was not able to move in with one or other of her informants. Nevertheless, both our researchers gained understanding by personal experience of what it means for a woman to work in the retail trade these days. Though each of the main three retail firms we studied differs in historic background, business philosophy and trading pattern, in all of them women make up the overwhelming majority of employees. Our studies, therefore, outline how female sales staff cope with the conflicting demands made on them in three different types of retail institutions. Before Kate Crehan and Annemarie Gerzer began their field studies we made sure that the management, staff and the trade unions concerned were fully informed of the objectives of our study and understood what it was all about.

Rather than depend solely on quantitative surveys, ours relies heavily on qualitative data. Kate Crehan, Scarlett Epstein and Annmarie Gerzer conducted many in-depth interviews with selected informants (1), mostly in their own homes. Our analysis makes extensive use of quotes from what our informants told us. In this way these individual employees rather than remain an impersonal statistic come to life.

Our German researchers, however, did make use of a lengthy questionnaire with many attitudinal questions which was distributed to over 500 members of the Beck staff in Munich. They offered a small payment for every questionnaire returned to compensate for the time the respondent spent in completing it. They had an almost 100 percent success rate with these questionnaires. Though our German studies have thus yielded also a considerable amount of quantitative information, they too rely in their analysis heavily on qualitative data. We maintain that such data offers much more meaningful and powerful illustrations of specific problem areas than can ever be achieved by means of quantification, although of course we also realise the importance of relevant statistics and use them wherever appropriate.

## THE MACRO-POLITICAL SETTING OF FAMILY AND WORK ISSUES: GREAT BRITAIN AND WEST GERMANY

The industrial revolution with its emphasis on monetary transactions brought with it a new kind of formal and spatial separation between domestic activities and productive work. Since then women have come to be regarded as solely responsible for running the home, an activity which has only low prestige while men have become the 'breadwinners' who are gainfully employed at a place outside their home which warrants high prestige. Industrialisation thus brought a 'significant shift in the relationship between work and the family. The new relationship, with its increased separation between these two areas of life, came to be incorporated in the "cognitive maps" of ordinary people. The world of work was perceived increasingly as a man's world - tough, competitive, heartless, while the home was women's territory - emotional, warm, supportive' (Moss, 1980:10). It is hardly necessary to point out that these general assumptions have never been fully reflected in practice.

The maternal role of women has always played an important part in the way society has seen and defined women. However, women do not always define themselves in this way. While certain allowances obviously have to be made for them in their role as mothers, many of them also have other aspirations besides producing and caring for their offspring. The stereotype of a woman, according to which she is happy to do nothing else but run her home and look after her family, has come to exercise a stranglehold over the improvement in the quality of life in industrialised countries in general and the possibility of increased job satisfaction for women in particular.

The all-exclusive emphasis on work accompanying the Industrial Revolution was further sanctioned by the Protestant ethic, which gives work a religious connotation. Work became an end in itself rather than a means to ensuring a better life all round. To this day society still defines the value of individuals on the basis of what they contribute to the gross national product, which significantly has always, and still continues, to include only monetary transactions. Men and women themselves define their respective values accordingly. Because of this, men's formal employment which can readily be quantified in monetary terms has continued to be awarded higher prestige than the domestic activities performed mainly by women, with which no monetary value is associated.

'The division of labor between the sexes defines to a certain extent the horizon within which the design of men's and women's lives is formulated; it also provides the respective contours of their lives' (Beck-Gernsheim, 1980:24). Any change in the division of labour between females and males, therefore, affects the total pattern of social life.

Governmental policies still appear to ignore the important contribution women make to the productive activities in industrialised countries. If all employed women would jointly decide to come out on strike the economy would immediately grind to a standstill. Moreover, women's work is not important only in its directly productive aspect but also in terms of the unpaid welfare services they provide, which relieve the pressure on official expenditures, a fact that still goes unnoticed by Governments. Childcare is not the only welfare activity women perform; care for the aged is becoming an increasingly heavy burden on women.

Recent British Governments have tended to shed their welfare responsibilities and women have had to fill this breach and, Jurgen Sass argues, there have been similar moves on the part of the present West German Government (see p.110). In order to fulfil all this unpaid welfare service women often work part-time only:

> This has minimised the need for new childcare
> arrangements beyond the family and school
> (which continue to care for most children of
> working parents) but has maximised employment
> disadvantages, concentrating working mothers
> increasingly into poorly paid, low-skilled
> jobs, with few benefits or prospects (Moss,
> 1980:15).

The large majority of British working mothers depend
on informal arrangements to help them meet their
family responsibilities for their children and aged
kin:

> Among working mothers with pre-school children,
> in the official British survey made by Hunt,
> over 70 percent paid nothing for childcare.
> About two-thirds listed a husband or other
> relatives as taking care of the children while
> they worked; most of them worked only part-
> time. About six percent of the children under
> two years old were in day nurseries, and about
> 12 percent of the three and four year olds were
> in nursery schools (Galenson, 1973:43).

By contrast in the Federal Republic of Germany
formal childcare facilities are more readily available. In 1981, 1,400,000 children benefited from
one or other formal care arrangement; only 20,000
children whose parents sought childcare for them
failed to be accommodated (Bundesminister fur
Jugend, Familie und Gesundheit, 1984:57). This
reflects the success of greater political pressures
from the 'Work and Family' lobby in West Germany
than in Great Britain. These great pressures in
West Germany also resulted in the creation of a
Federal Ministry for Youth, Family and Health
(Bundesministerium fur Jugend, Familie und
Gesundheit).
    Altogether Great Britain is one of the few EEC
countries without a ministry specifically concerned
with family matters. The West German Ministry
sponsors a great deal of research on present and
future patterns of work and family life; it also
brings out a series of publications in this field of
which Familie und Arbeitswelt (Family and the World
of Work) Volume 143, is a notable recent addition.
    In Great Britain, too, there have been an in-
creasing number of publications by Her Majesty's
Stationary Office, which focus on women, of which
Women and Employment, a Life Time Perspective, 1984

is the most recent. These reports, however, are mainly statistical and leave untouched the qualitative problems of time management at work and at home. There is therefore in Great Britain no attempt yet made by Governmental efforts to link work with family life and view these as two interacting spheres of social life. This is of course understandable in view of the lack of a Ministry specifically concerned with family and work matters.

Significantly, our German study was conducted by the German Youth Institute (Deutsches Jugendinstitut) which is financed by the Federal Ministry for Youth, Family and Health. By contrast, our British study was directed by T. Scarlett Epstein of the University of Sussex who, together with Kate Crehan, conducted it as part of their personally chosen research assignments. While our West German study thus has official support and sanction, our British study remains outside the governmental sphere of interest. This indicates the major difference in the political setting of working women that exists in the two countries. The Government of the Federal Republic of Germany appears to be altogether more concerned with 'quality of life issues' than are British Governments. Family and Work Issues in these two countries thus have to be viewed against this macropolitical background.


BUSINESS PHILOSOPHIES

The optimisation of profits is generally considered the major objective of all business ventures in Western industrial societies. Yet within this overall uniform setting there seems ample room for variation. Each of the three retail institutions we studied (two in Great Britain and one in West Germany) operates with a different business philosophy. The BCS trading exercise gives its shareholders and consumers prime consideration. It claims to be the retail institution that 'shares and cares'; it shares with its shareholders and cares for its customers. There is nothing in the institutional structure of the BCS to insure a concern with industrial relations, except of course that it has a Personnel Department. The BCS operates 80 separate retail outlets of which the Peacehaven Superstore is only one. Since staff is not obliged, nor even encouraged to become shareholders, only few employees at Peacehaven hold BCS shares. The majority of them regard working there as they would working anywhere else, without feeling any specific involvement or commitment to the BCS. This is reflected in a high labour turnover rate.

Roberts Bros. is a long established department store which has always stressed the importance of good relations between staff and management; an emphasis reflected in a relatively low turnover of staff. But it too operated under the same pressure to continually increase the productivity of its employees.

Beck, the Munich department store we studied, more resembles Roberts Bros in its managerial practices than it does the BCS. Beck has taken a step further the harmonious industrial relations which seem to exist at Roberts Bros As an old family business it has always cared for employees who therefore felt that they could approach management with their family problems. More recently the Beck motto is that the 'customer is host rather than king', which gives a new dimension to retailing. It changes the relationship between sales personnel and customers from subordination to a friendly one where the two parties operate on an equal footing. Annemarie Gerzer found a high work commitment among staff. The job identity among Beck's staff is further reinforced by the 'indiviudual work-time' scheme (see pp.119-121) the firm introduced some years ago. 'Individual work time' offers even more flexibility to employees than does flexitime. However, Annemarie Gerzer stresses that the success of this system depends on the managerial style of individual department heads (see p.154). Employees in each department who come under the 'individual work time' arrangements can within limits choose when and for what periods they come to work. This highly flexible employment structure is welcomed by each and every one who works accordingly. It also, of course, encounters a number of problems, which are discussed by Gertzer.

Beck's management continues to encourage further the job identity among their employees with a staff policy that promotes the self-expression of individual staff members and is based on the assumption that the work environment can and should promote individual self-fulfillment. It should be noted though that the 'Beck Model' is not representative of business philosophy and practice followed by other department stores in West Germany.

As yet Beck is a fairly unique 'avant garde' type of department store. Though its novel business philosophy and consequently different type of management-staff relations seem at first sight to offer most of the solutions to the problem of time management at work and at home experienced by many female employees, it is important to stress that it does not provide the panacea in this context. It has several drawbacks, the most important of which is the self-selection of the categories of its female staff. Women with pre-school or even young school going children hardly have a chance to get a job at Beck. This is because the greatest demand for sales services occurs usually over the lunch hours, when neither childcare facilities nor schools are open to look after children (2). Therefore, implicitly the Beck style operation makes it difficult for young mothers of small children who often most need the flexibility which 'individual work time' has to offer, to find employment. Only 6 percent of the women who are employed under the 'individual work time' system are young married mothers of children below the age of ten (see p.145). Needs of these young women are not accommodated by the management. Moreover, though its novel business philosophy promotes full job identity among sales staff, in terms of power relations between management and staff Beck is not really much different from most other retail businesses. Yet its success in introducing a flexible work pattern in line with staff and customers' requirements, together with its continuingly growing turnover, indicates that concern for staff satisfaction does not necessarily conflict with an emphasis on profitability, but can be mutually re-enforcing.

## 'REAL WORK', 'DOMESTIC WORK' AND THE FAMILY

As already mentioned, most working women are first and foremost committed to their families. Women's domestic work is of course also socially productive in as much as it contributes to the reproduction and maintenance of labour:

> The productiveness of domestic work is, however, obscured by the fact that it is performed in privatised family units. The result of this privatisation is that the domestic worker appears to be performing a personal service for the family, whereas industrial work is seen to be socially productive. In terms of this comparison

domestic work does not seem to be a real job at all (Hunt, 1980:111).

This helps to explain why women who are not in formal employment, but who work jolly hard looking after their home and numbers of small children, still usually say no if asked whether they are 'working'.

Work outside the home has gained such overriding importance in industrial societies that self-respect makes most individuals want to perform directly productive work outside their place of residence. This helps to explain why women are prepared to go through what Kate Crehan calls the 'balancing act' in order to assure themselves of a self-identity. However, most women have to choose between job satisfaction and a family at least during part of their working lives, a choice which men have to make only rarely. On the other hand, men are generally deprived of the pleasures which come with bringing up children. Changes in the relationship between work and family life may thus benefit not only women but also men. The perception of gender roles, however, seems so deeply embedded in our culture that it is likely to change only slowly.

Our studies focussed on women in gainful employment only; more research is needed to discover the self-image and aspirations of those working-class women who remain full-time housewives. What makes them accept their status as second-class citizens? And what are their aspirations? Without answers to these questions it is difficult to understand the full depth of the 'time management problem' which working women face in their daily lives.

What does emerge clearly from our studies though is the greater job commitment amongst our German, as compared with our British, female informants. The novel business philosophy which the Beck department store is pioneering has a lot to do with this. However, there is another factor which is also important in this context. This is the different educational patterns that exist in Great Britain and West Germany in general and the vocational training for sales staff in West Germany in particular, and the lack of it in Great Britain.

VOCATIONAL QUALIFICATION AND SELF-ESTEEM

The West German educational pattern puts greater emphasis on vocational qualifications not only for skilled but also for unskilled and/or semi-skilled jobs than is the case in Great Britain. Two or three years apprenticeship coupled with appropriate vocational education is a common feature in most occupations in West Germany. About two thirds of all pupils in secondary education are being prepared for one or other occupation. The large majority of them go straight into a job on leaving school, but begin work by serving several years apprenticeship usually associated with appropriate formal vocational education. At the end of the apprenticeship period, and when individuals have passed the required examinations, they are generally regarded as 'master craftsmen'. This lengthy training ensures higher productivity per labour day. Moreover the title of 'master craftsman' carries considerable prestige which is reflected in greater job commitment among those who are thus qualified.

The British educational system has undergone radical restructuring particularly since the last war, but the elitism in the British educational system still manifests itself in the low prestige that is attached to applied versus theoretical studies.

Apprenticeship in Great Britain is generally associated only with a limited number of specified occupations. No more than 19 percent of males and 13 percent females aged 16 to 18 were attending recognised vocational courses in 1982. The respective percentages for men and women aged 19-20 were nine and three percent (DES, 1984:3). By contrast in West Germany vocational training is far more widely spread over the whole spectrum of work. There about 77 pecent of all gainfully employed men and 62 percent of all gainfully employed women have an occupational qualification acquired by means of either on job training linked with vocational education or vocational education only.

Almost all West German females engaged in the retail trade have finished two or three years vocational training and education. Female retail apprentices constituted almost 21 percent of all German apprentices in 1981. In Great Britain being a shop assistant is generally regarded as a job that requires no skill whatsoever. Accordingly, school boys and girls aged fourteen and over are frequently employed as part-time shop assistants to meet the peak customer demand usually at week-ends.

## FLEXIBLE WORK PATTERNS

Nothing epitomises the impact of domestic responsibilities on women's working lives more than the amount of time women with varying domestic commitments work during the week and the times of day when they work. For many women, this issue is crucial in determining whether they take paid employment at all and indeed "convenient hours" often takes priority over all other aspects of a job (Martin, 1984:34).

Not surprisingly, by far the majority of part-time workers are women. Trade Unions still seem to regard part-timers as a threat to improved working conditions for full-timers. This is understandable in Great Britain where most part-timers still operate outside the legal protection which full-timers enjoy.

In West Germany, too, the trade unions oppose the expansion of part-time work and instead advocate reduction in the working week as if these two alternatives were necessarily mutually exclusive options (see p.114). Both the British and the German studies indicate the high priority flexibility has for women workers, and Annemarie Gerzer discusses this at great length (see Part III). Joy Kuhn, a till operator for the BCS, in her own account pleads for more flexibility as far as working hours are concerned. Management 'could be a bit more flexible about letting people make up time they have missed because they had to stay home with a sick child or whatever... They should automatically be paid the same and just make up the hours some other time' (see p.169). On her own initiative Joy Kuhn thus suggests a scheme similar to the 'individual work time' operating at the Beck department store.

"Convenient hours" are an absolutely crucial requirement for part-time workers, for, if the hours are not right, women wanting to combine employment and their domestic responsibilities cannot work at all. The consequence of this is that part-time workers often make certain trade-offs, attaching less importance to a "good rate of pay" than to "convenient hours" even when they work "mainly for money" (Martin,

1984:188).

The plight of female part-timers thus urgently needs attention by the Trade Unions to ensure that they are not subjected to lower working conditions just because employers are prepared to offer them 'convenient working hours'.

Our studies illustrate the urgent need for increasing flexibility in work patterns both inside and outside the home - to help reduce the conflict so many women presently face between job and family commitments. This necessitates an innovative attitude all round by management, staff and trade unions. We found the two main British retail stores we studied more tradition-bound than Beck the Munich department store. Beck has not only successfully introduced 'job sharing' on a departmental basis with its 'individual work time', but is also experimenting with job sharing among some of its female managerial staff (see p.176). Neither the BCS nor Roberts Bros. are as yet prepared even to consider job sharing a feasible proposition. Job sharing is of course not the only way to increase work flexibility for women. There are a number of other options in this field, which need to be explored. The main advantage Beck offers is willingness to experiment and innovate. Though Beck has not gone far enough yet in its innovative practices it seems to be moving in the right direction.

Women's ongoing search for a dual identity and the 'balancing act' that this involves poses a challenge to industrial societies which, unless successfully met, will be to the detriment not only of the quality of life of present populations but even more so of future generations.


NOTES

1. The names given to our informants in the text are pseudonyms to hide their real identity. In the chapter 'male managers' and 'female employees' Scarlett Epstein also drew on some interviews with managers in stores other than the BCS Superstore and Roberts Bros.

2. Most nurseries in West Germany only function in the mornings and so do all schools.

Chart 1.1: Who Does What? (Great Britain)

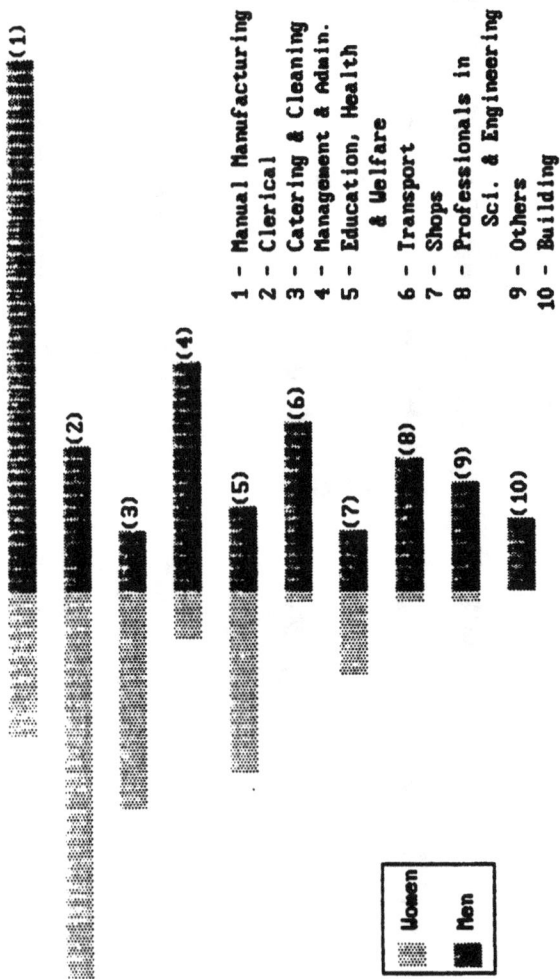

1 – Manual Manufacturing
2 – Clerical
3 – Catering & Cleaning
4 – Management & Admin.
5 – Education, Health
    & Welfare
6 – Transport
7 – Shops
8 – Professionals in
    Sci. & Engineering
9 – Others
10 – Building

(1) (2) (3) (4) (5) (6) (7) (8) (9) (10)

Women
Men

Source: H.M. Governments 'New Earnings Survey' (1982)

Chart 1.2: Who Does What? (West Germany)

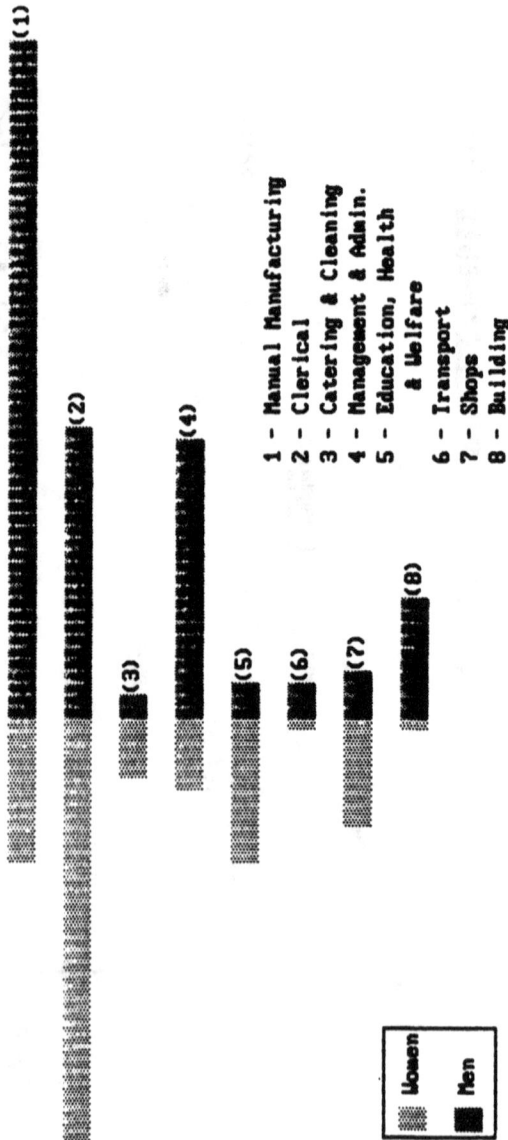

1 – Manual Manufacturing
2 – Clerical
3 – Catering & Cleaning
4 – Management & Admin.
5 – Education, Health
     & Welfare
6 – Transport
7 – Shops
8 – Building

(1) (2) (3) (4) (5) (6) (7) (8)

Women
Men

Source: Wirtschaft und Statistik 5/1984
        pp.414–416 Ergebnisse des Mikrozensus (1982)

# PART TWO

## WOMEN IN THE RETAIL TRADE
## (GREAT BRITAIN)

Chapter 2

WOMEN, WORK AND THE BALANCING ACT (1)

Kate Crehan

THE SETTING: SUPERSTORE AND DEPARTMENT STORE

The two case studies carried out in Britain involved
two very different sections of the retail trade.
The first and major study was of a Superstore in a
new shopping precinct in Peacehaven, a small town
just outside Brighton; the second and much shorter
study was of a long established department store in
the centre of a big city. The main research method
used in both studies was participant observation
with myself as the sole researcher. For the Superstore study I spent six months in the store, working
at different times in all its main sections. During
this time I lived in the home of one of the women
employed in the store. For the department store
study I worked for a month in a single department.
During the time I was working in the two stores I
tried, as far as possible, to carry out all the
duties of any ordinary employee. In both stores I
also interviewed a small number of women - 23 at the
department store and ten at the Superstore - in more
depth.(2) These interviews were not based on a
questionnaire and although I did have a set range of
topics which were covered in each interview, the
interviews were allowed to range very freely.
        The retail trade as a whole has undergone con-
siderable upheaval and reorganisation in recent
years and the two case studies represent two different ways of adapting to the hard realities of
modern retailing. The department store as we know
it today developed at the end of the last century
and was itself a response to the demands of a new
and changing market. But however pioneering in
their heyday, nowadays department stores are increasingly beleaguered. They face growing competition
from the multiple chain stores with their massive

purchasing power and their consequent ability to cut
prices to the bone, the new shopping precincts with
their easy access and lavish parking facilities, and
the whole gamut of shops and markets designed for
the new type of shopper who is less and less likely
to be the kind of customer the traditional department store was designed around: the full-time,
middle-class housewife with time on her hands and
money to spend (Jeffries, 1954:329). In a time of
general economic recession with a static, or even
declining population, competition becomes ever more
cut-throat and there is less and less space for the
old-time department store; only the fittest are
likely to survive. Roberts Bros, the department
store where I carried out my brief study, is one of
those which is not only surviving, but actually
prospering. This is due in part to the fact that
Roberts Bros is part of a large group of department
stores that has itself adopted a number of the
characteristics of the multiple chain-store giants.

The group has a policy of offering competitive
prices and yet at the same time still providing the
kind of personal service traditionally associated
with department stores - there is, for instance, a
free local delivery service for customers. Unlike
the subject of the German case study, Beck, Roberts
Bros does not set itself up as being ultra fashion-
able; it is not in the business of selling whole
lifestyles, it aims to be seen rather as the store
where you can buy anything and everything, whatever
direction your tastes lie in. As I was told by both
managers and sales staff, what they believe their
customers feel is, 'Well, I thought if I can't get
it at Roberts Bros then I can't get it anywhere.'

One of the developments in retailing which has
made life more difficult for the traditional department store has been the increasing number of superstores and the way the big food retailers are increasingly tending to use such stores to move into
non-food selling. The shopper whose needs the Superstore is geared around is the car and deep-freezer
owner who has a limited amount of time for shopping.
The Superstore which was chosen for the study
embodies many of the major trends in modern retailing.

It is large, covering an area of 45,000 square
feet and employing almost 200 staff and is located
in a purpose-built shopping centre some distance
away from traditional shopping areas, with extensive
parking facilities. The store is organised on a
self-service basis with a minimum of sales staff;

sales and cash-flow are monitored by a computer; and stock control and ordering are intended to be compu- terised eventually. There is a high percentage of female employees and a high percentage of part- timers - at the time of my fieldwork 64 percent of employees were women and 53 percent of all employees were part-timers. The store sells both food and non- food stuffs - approximately 80 percent of the store's sales area is given over to food and 20 percent to non-foods. Apart from a large grocery section, the food sections include fresh fruit and vegetables, fresh meat, a delicatessen, wines and spirits, and a wide range of frozen foods. The non- food sections include general hardware, electrical goods, shoes, a small range of clothes, sports goods, toys, records and tape cassettes.

The store is owned by the Brighton Co-operative Society (BCS) and is its first Superstore. Peacehaven, the small but rapidly expanding town where the store is located, is something of a new community; taking Peacehaven and the adjoining area of Telscombe - once separate communities but now to all intents and purposes forming a single unity - together the population has grown from 13,190 in 1971 to 15,439 in 1981, nearly 80 percent of whom live in owner-occupied housing with 68 percent of households (OPCS Monitor, 1984) owning a car (1981 Census). Peacehaven/Telscombe has one shopping centre, the Meridian Centre, a recently built com- plex of shops and small factory units which is still in the final stages of completion. As far as grocery and general food shops within Peacehaven are con- cerned, the Superstore enjoys a near monopoly. Its only competitors are a few small, virtual one-man businesses. Within the Meridian Centre, as well as the Superstore, the BCS has a pharmacy and a Do-It- Yourself and gardening shop. A high percentage of the men who live in Peacehaven work outside the area, in Brighton, Newhaven or even further afield; there are not many opportunities for employment within Peacehaven and the Superstore is one of the few big employers of labour. When I asked people why they lived in Peacehaven, the usual reason I was given was the relative cheapness of houses compared to elsewhere in the area, and its pleasant rural environment.

TWO PHILOSOPHIES

Underlying the Peacehaven Superstore and Roberts

Bros are two somewhat different philosophies, each a
historical legacy and each with their own political
implications for the lives of employees. The BCS,
which owns and runs the Peacehaven Superstore, is
part of a powerful historical tradition. All
accounts of the Co-operative movement start with the
Rochdale pioneers and the warehouse in Toad Lane
which in 1844 they converted into a shop to be run
for the benefit of its customers rather than simply
to generate profits (Co-operative Retail Services
Limited n.d:1). The Co-op has become a huge multi-
faceted organisation with banks, an insurance company, printing press, travel agencies, funeral par-
lours in addition to 7,000 shops, but this colossal
empire is still made up of 120 separate and quite
independent regional societies such as the BCS. All
Co-operative Societies still adhere to the principles laid down by the Rochdale pioneers. To this
day they still focus primarily on consumers, and are
based on the principle that it is the Society's
customers who should receive any profits generated;
in no sense were these commercial ventures ever
worker co-operatives. The Co-operative movement
was founded during the decade that became known as
'the hungry forties'; a time of particular hardship
for the working class. Although the infamous truck
system, whereby employers forced their workers to
buy from company shops selling shoddy goods at in-
flated prices, had recently been legislated against,
finding decent quality at fair prices was still a
problem for working-class shoppers (Cole, 1945).
Most shops were geared around the needs of the
middle-class shopper and the exponential growth of
the Co-operative movement can be seen as a response
to the particular needs of working-class shoppers
for whom other shops were not catering. The warm
memories of many older people for the Co-ops of
their youth is a testament to the way the Co-op
movement went on serving the needs of working-
class communities throughout much of this century.
    Rose, who worked at the Superstore, remembered
the Co-ops of her youth as very much geared around
the needs of a working-class clientele:

> You got mainly working-class people at the Co-
> op then... and people with plenty of money went
> to more high-class places, and you know, got
> the better food. No, the Co-op was definitely
> for the people and, of course, the dividend,
> that little bit of extra money they got. Also,
> they did vouchers: you could buy two, three, or

>      four pounds worth of these vouchers which you
>      paid 4s (3) a week back, something like that,
>      if it was four pounds it was 4s, if it was five
>      pounds it was 5s; and they were done in 5s
>      units so you could just tear one off and spend
>      5s. I can remember when I first went out to
>      work my mother got a two pound voucher for me
>      to go and get a new coat, and I had to pay this
>      money back so that was 2s out of my wages.

This was a long time before hire-purchase schemes
became widely available, at a time when credit was
always something of a problem for working-class
consumers. It was always, however, as consumers
rather than as employees that workers benefited from
the Co-op.
    Over the years the growing importance of wor-
kers as consumers, has meant that they are no
longer, as consumers, the beleaguered and ignored
group they used to be; they are a valuable prize to
be courted and wooed by all the struggling conten-
ders in the retail world. At the same time many
workers now have cars and deep-freezers. In
essence, the particular role the old time Co-op
fulfilled, located within working-class communities
and serving the specific need of these communities,
has disappeared and, if they are to survive, modern
Co-operative Societies, like modern department
stores, must adapt to the new world of modern
retailing; but where does this leave the principles
of the Rochdale pioneers? In their determination
to adapt the modern Co-operative Societies often run
stores that are indistinguishable from those of
their capitalist competitors, such as Sainsbury's,
'except that Sainsbury's are more efficient', to
quote one representative of a small Co-op battling
against the modernising tide (Guardian, 26.5.84).
It is in the context of these kinds of issues and
questions that the BCS Superstore at Peacehaven
needs to be situated.
    The BCS employs 1,800 people in its various
enterprises and has an annual turnover of more than
50 million pounds. Like other Co-operative Societies, many of its shops are small and all too often
in modern conditions that means uneconomic. For the
BCS, as for so many in the retail trade, the Superstore is the shop of the future so that, as I was
often told, the Peacehaven Superstore is the BCS's
flagship; and, as the Society's first Superstore, it
is something of a test case, the progress of which
is being closely monitored.

When I began my research in Peacehaven one of
the first questions I was interested in was whether
or not this Co-op Superstore was in fact different
from Sainsbury's, Asda and the rest, either in terms
of its relationship to its customers, or to its
employees. Basically in both cases the answer
seems to be no. The Co-op's slogan may be 'the
people who care', but in fact, since above all the
Superstore must be a viable economic proposition, it
is forced, quite independently of any 'co-operative
ideals' the individuals running the Society may
have, to operate according to the same hard-nosed
economic rationality as its private enterprise competitors; its care for its customers comes down to a
care that it offers the kind of prices, range of
goods, shopping hours and other facilities that will
ensure enough paying customers pass through its
check-outs. The narrow profit margins it is forced
to operate within mean that even that most characteristic feature of Co-op shopping the 'divi' - or
nowadays the dividend stamp - is not given in the
Superstore.

While the co-operative element of the Co-op was
always concerned primarily with its customers rather
than those it employed, at the same time Co-
operative Societies like to think of themselves as
'good' employers who treat their workers as well as
the best of their competitors. All Co-operative
Societies have a post entry closed shop agreement
with the Union of the Shop, Distributive and Allied
Workers (USDAW), which means that all employees must
join the Union. Some of the reality of being employed in the BCS's Superstore will emerge, I hope,
in the course of this chapter, but the basic
constraints of a need to keep labour costs to a
minimum applies as much to the Co-op as to any other
retail organisation. In general, all the employees
of the Superstore agreed that there was no real
difference between the BCS and any other big store
in terms of the way they treated their employees;
the only difference was that there were some firms,
the usual example cited was Marks and Spencer,
which in certain respects was thought to treat their
workers a good deal better than the BCS.

The philosophy on which Roberts Bros is based
is very different to that of the Co-op. As a long-
established, family-run firm it claims to have a
special relationship with its staff, many of whom
stay with the company for longer than is usual in
the retail trade. A few years ago staff with over
five years service were brought into a share option

scheme, giving them a vested interest in the success
of the business and, as the management put it,
rewarding them for their loyalty.
But at the end of the day, as the cliche has
it, the harsh material reality of the need to remain
a viable business enterprise remains, and it is the
constraints imposed by this harsh reality, rather
than a particular philosophical outlook, that deter-
mines the basic shape of both Peacehaven Superstore
and Roberts Bros. Crucially, for instance, there is
the same relentless pressure to keep staff costs
down which necessarily means either cutting down on
the number of staff employed or paying those that
are employed less. At the same time the store must
still be able to provide an adequate level of service for customers.

## MORAL DIVISIONS OF LABOUR: THE WORK ETHIC AND THE MATERNAL ETHIC

Both the Superstore and Roberts Bros belong to
large organisations which must operate within constraints deriving from the nature of the retail
trade in general. Each organisation has a long history behind it, and each bears many traces of that
history: Like institutions, individuals are the
joint products of history and present realities. In
terms of mental structures, one of the most important ways in which a particular group of individuals
can be seen to belong to a particular historical
moment is in as much as they share a whole set of
assumptions and beliefs about the nature of the
reality in which they live. In no sense does this
complicated bundle form a coherent and consistent
whole; all of us are capable of holding many contradictory ideas simply because our different ideas are
brought out in different contexts, and consequently
their inconsistency is never a problem. Many of the
most powerful beliefs that people hold - powerful
that is in the sense of determining the kinds of
choices they make in the course of their lives - are
all the taken-for-granted, often unstated assumptions which rather than being argued about tend to
be taken as 'facts' which can be used to back up
arguments. Given the particular social realities of
a particular historical time and place there are
bound to be assumptions which appear to be self-
evident unchangeable 'facts' because they do indeed
follow directly from those specific social realities. As social realities change, so too will social

norms, although not in an automatic and mechanical way; different ways of articulating new realities are always struggled over and there may be a considerable time lag before a new norm succeeds in embedding itself as an established truth.

One of the social realities anyone who has a paid job faces is the demand that they fufil both their family commitments and those of their job. The way in which people manage their time between home and work is not simply a quantitative question of how long they spend doing this or that task, it also has a fundamental qualitative dimension which is concerned with the nature and form of certain moral obligations and commitments. In order to understand this qualitative dimension it is helpful to delve a little into some of the underlying structures of belief, and into the social realities that continually recreate them.

Modern industrial society creates two distinct and opposed domains: the public domain of social production and work for wages, and the private, unwaged domain of family and home. Work done in the home, however arduous and however necessary to the wellbeing of the family members, is not paid employment and so does not count as real work. For instance when I asked Laura if her mother had worked when she, Laura, was a child, she said, 'No, my mother never worked,' only after a pause did she go on to add, 'I say this, she did have a boarding house... (she) worked jolly hard as well.' It is understood that asking a housewife if she works is asking her if she has got a job outside the home. The fact that these two domains are ideological constructs rather than factual descriptions does not make them any the less important.

At one level individuals who go out to work, whether they are men or women, are faced with conflicting demands on their time: how do they budget their time between work and home? But there is also the whole level of the beliefs and assumptions individuals have about the nature of their moral obligations, and their relationships in general to work and to home; how should they budget their time? It is this level I am chiefly concerned with in this section since these deep undercurrents play such an important role in shaping the way individuals not only deal with, but actually perceive the objective conditions that confront them. Tracing out the different threads in this complex mental knot, and following through the linkages between them is a complicated business, not least because the whole area is shot through with so many powerful and deeply internalised moral imperatives. While it is often argued that the 'work ethic' is losing its moral force, paid employment is still the most powerful source, whether positive or negative, of self-identity in any industrial society; and what could be called the 'maternal ethic' that is the belief that a mother's primary and most important responsibility is to her children, is so taken for granted that it is seldom even stated explicitly.

## THE MORAL BALANCING ACT

Although the domains of work and home may be thought of as separate, all real individuals with jobs necessarily and simultaneously inhabit both. Using both data from my interviews, and data collected in the course of working in the Superstore and the department store, I want to take a few specific examples of the ways in which individual women see their own particular balancing act between work and home, and to probe a little into what lies behind certain of their statements.

All the women I spoke to accepted as a basic fact of life that family - particularly children - and a career represent competing options for women:

> I don't know how women work a career with children. I think it's got to be one or the other. I just don't see how you can work the two together. (MAY)

> I wouldn't leave my children with anybody to do a job, that's why I find the Co-op so useful to do the evening work. So then my husband's here all the time and that way I don't have to worry about the children being looked after by any-body... If the Co-op wasn't there then I wouldn't work because I wouldn't leave the children. (EILEEN)

> I think if you get married, you have a family, well that's your first consideration. If you want to keep a career, I don't think you should get married... if you get married they come first and your job comes second. (ROSE)

Often the demands of the family, and most im-portantly of children, were seen as inevitably ruling out most jobs at least until the children

Women, Work and the Balancing Act

have left school.  A recurrent theme was the determination  that children should not come home  to  an
empty house.  For  example when I went on  to  ask
Eileen about her future work plans,  would she,  for
instance,  get a full-time job when her children are
a bit older, she said:

> Probably  not  until  they (the  children)  are
> grown  up  because they have got  their  school
> life  until  16  or 17 so they will  still  be
> coming  home and I wouldn't want them  to  come
> home to an empty house. (EILEEN)

Another woman, who does not as yet have children but
would  like  to,  stressed that although  she  would
consider  a part-time job when they start  going  to
school,  'I'm  a  firm believer that when the  child
comes home from school a parent should be there.   I
don't  believe  in  kids coming  back  to  an  empty
house.' (ELLEN)

'I  feel  I've  had the kids so I  should  look
after  them and that's it,' (JO).   'You can't expect
other people to look after your responsibility (i.e.
your  children)' (MARJORIE).   In general it  is  so
taken for granted that the primary moral responsibility  for a child's wellbeing falls inescapably  on
the  mother that this seldom has to be stated explicitly,  it  is simply a moral truth structuring  the
whole  way women perceive the options  available  to
them.   I say women here, because it does not simply
structure  the  identity  of  mothers.  One  of  the
central  ideological  components of the  meaning  of
being  a  woman is being a  mother; a woman  who  is
unable  to bear children is an object of pity while a
woman  who chooses not to have children is seen as a
bit  odd,  not a 'proper' woman, so that whether it is
an  actual  or merely potential role as mother,  it is
the  moral obligations inherent in this role that are
seen  as structuring the way a woman,  any woman - in
as  much as she is defined as a woman  - necessarily
perceives  the  priorities in her  life.   In  other
words,  at  a very deep ideological level,  being  a
woman and being a worker necessarily make  conflicting  demands which will tend,  and according to  the
deepest  moral  imperatives,  ought  to be resolved in
favour  of the demands of the family.   At the  same
time there is another deeply internalised ideological  assumption in modern industrial society that  a
full  social identity involves some sort of role  as
worker and that the only real work is that work that

32

is paid for. For individuals what this means is a
sense that not having a job is somehow morally
wrong; and even if this is rejected at a rational
level it can be difficult to break free emotionally.
The work ethic still remains a powerful force. As a
result there is often a profound ambivalence underlying the answers women give to questions about work
and home. The following extract from one of my
interviews is interesting in that it shows a young
unmarried girl of 17, still living at home, who has
not yet had to cope with the contradictions in
practice, trying to combine a number of contradictory norms into some coherent whole. The girl,
Sharon, is attractive and slightly tomboyish. She
often says how she prefers the company of men, where
she feels she can fit in, to that of women who she
sees as inherently bitchy. She wants to get married
eventually but she intends to have a good time
first. I asked her if she would work when she got
married to which she replied:

SHARON  Yes. I'll go on working because I believe that everything should be equal so I think
that if the man brings in money why shouldn't the
female, but then when I have a child, then I expect
to look after the kid until its school age and then
I'll get myself a part-time job until it's old
enough to look after itself, and then I'll go out
and get full-time work unless I have another one.
KATE  Would you like a career?
SHARON  Oh, yes I know what I'm going to do,
you know.
KATE  What do you want to do?
SHARON  I want to do rehabilitation with handicapped teenagers, my age, teach them how to look
after themselves, how to do the sort of things that
you do in the home, basic home life, how to look
after yourself in the home on your own, which half
of them haven't got a clue how to do. That's what I
went to Tech for, and if I can't do that then I want
to look after elderly people and as far as I'm
concerned that is a career.

I went on to probe a little deeper into just how
Sharon saw herself combining a career and family.
She was quite clear both that the needs of her
children would be paramount and that her work schedule would have to fit in with these needs. In this
context the only obligation she saw as possibly
overruling these needs was that of straight financial necessity.

   SHARON  If I was that desperate for money  then
I'd  try  to get friends to look after the kids  but
I'd  try  and arrange it when the kids came  out  of
school  I'd  look after the kids,  I'd  be  at  home
waiting  for  them... I  wouldn't send  them  to  a
stranger, I wouldn't do that.

Sharon  was like most of the women I interviewed  in
that  her ideal career involved the accepted  female
role of homemaking and caring for others.   The work
histories of most of the young women I interviewed -
or  in  case of some of the very young  girls  their
work aspirations - involved some kind of nursing  or
other  caring job or another archetypal female  job,
hairdressing.  Later  in the interview with Sharon,
however,  another aspiration emerged which seems  to
indicate some ambivalence as regards her own definition of herself.  She was quite emphatic that it was
only  the different ways men and women were  brought
up  that  explain  any differences in  the  kind  of
skills each sex acquires.

   SHARON  If  you reversed it around and we  were
brought up like fellas and they were brought up like
us then we'd be like them.  As far as I'm concerned
I  wouldn't mind working on a building site...  I'd
love to be a lorry driver.  Females can do it,  I'd
rather work with handicapped  and elderly because  I
don't think enough people look at handicapped people
and think,  "Oh,  they're human beings", they think,
"Oh,  that's a handicap, what's that?" which I think
is  unfair.   Also  I think that I've got  something
more than them... when I'm older I can have a home,
have  a family and raise kids,  where they can't  do
that,  because they haven't got a clue some of them,
they've  led such secluded lives,  they  just  don't
know how to do it... I feel sorry for them, I know I
shouldn't but  I  do,  I feel sorry they've  got  a
different life to able-bodied people... I think they
shouldn't...  I think they should have the same  way
of  life because they are no different half of  them
and they are so nice.  I'd love to be a lorry driver
and  unless something stops me,  when I'm 21 I shall
take my test to be a lorry driver.

One  of  the reasons for quoting this  interview  at
some length is that once again it brings out the way
an individual's stated beliefs, even when made in an
apparently  forceful and unambiguous way,  may  mask
considerable  ambiguity and contradiction,  particularly  where strong moral imperatives such as  those

defining the 'proper' female role are involved. It
also seems to me that in Sharon's case her obvious
empathy for the plight of the handicapped could be
related to a certain sense of alienation.
Another woman, Karen, also revealed another and
somewhat different underlying conflict in her self-
definition. Karen is a divorced woman of 38, who
lives alone with her 19-year-old daughter. She
works part-time in the office of the store. Karen
complained to me about the way some of her male
workmates teased her because she did not have and
did not want a boyfriend.

KATE   I think sometimes men feel threatened by
a woman who's free, who doesn't have a man con-
trolling her.
KAREN  Possibly, I don't know. And yet I've
never really been a career person, I've always been
a family person. It's circumstances have forced me
to do other things.
KATE   You would have always seen the centre of
your life as home and family.
KAREN  Yes definitely. I mean I would still
have liked to have worked perhaps... I would still
have taken on the job at the Co-op... especially
with my daughter leaving school and going out to
work, it would have been nice for me. But really
the job would have been secondary whereas now it has
to be the main thing because now I'm the breadwinner.

It is interesting here, I think, that Karen equates
my statement about women and freedom with a woman
having a career and immediately distances herself
from what she perceives as the role of a 'career
woman'. And when Karen says, 'But really the job
would have been secondary,' a little of the ideological underpinning of the cliche that women work
just for pin-money begins to be revealed. When it
is said that a woman works for pin-money, whether it
is said by the woman herself or is said about her,
often I would argue what is really being said has
much more to do with the way her job is seen, by
herself or by others, as fitting with the rest of
her life, than it has to do with the question of how
financially important her wages are to her. In
other words, saying that a woman works for pin-money
is, at one level, saying that her job neither plays
the same major role in defining her social identity
as it does in the case of a man nor constitutes the
source of such important moral responsibilities.

Later in the interview Karen provided a very clear example of the way peoples' definitions of themselves, their aspirations, and apparently deeply held convictions may in fact reflect the way they see the realities that confront them and their need, in the face of these realities, which we all share, to construct a self-image that is both acceptable and realistic. Karen talked about how tiring she found her job:

KAREN But there you are, I console myself with the fact that I'm lucky I've got a job that is convenient and is suitable in lots of ways, so you see I'm not really ambitious. If I was I'd leave, take this course (in typing) and think to hell with it. There again I lack confidence.
KATE When you say you are not really ambitious is that what you are really saying?
KAREN No, it's not. It's that I'm not really confident enough to do perhaps what I'd like to do.

There is, I suggest, a basic division of labour between the sexes at the level of fundamental moral obligations. The prevailing social norms locate the primary moral responsibility of women firmly within the sphere of home and family, and this in itself, quite apart from all the other barriers, sets up powerful psychological barriers which make it difficult for women to operate in the sphere of work in the same way that men do. Thus women often feel a profound ambivalence about their role as workers, while employers, and often unions, tend to be ambivalent about women's role in the workplace. ; But what of the male side of this equation, what are the equivalent structuring norms for male identity and what effects do they have? Men's primary moral obligations are located within the public sphere of work and social production. It is true that men are seen as having important responsibilities towards their families, but the 'proper' means by which their obligations to their families are met is by their participation in social production. Within the family a man's role is first and foremost that of breadwinner, and the family itself, particularly the wife, has the duty of supporting and servicing the man so that he is equipped to fulfil the role of breadwinner adequately. That is the ideology. But real men in the real world experience all kinds of conflicts between the demands made on them as workers and as husbands and fathers: whereas it is socially recognised that women with jobs characteri-

stically experience this kind of conflict, there is
not supposed to be the same inherent conflict in the
case of men. It is significant that the BCS, in
common with many other organisations, record their
female employees marital status on their personnel
cards but not the marital status of their male
employees. One of the practical effects of this
ideology is that women, and particularly mothers,
are often seen as being inherently unreliable as
employees because of their family obligations, but
although men too are late, and have to take time off
because of family obligations, such instances tend
to be seen simply as isolated incidents which have
no bearing on the way men with children are thought
of as workers.


HOMEMAKERS

Another important set of norms which shapes the way
women think of themselves and the options which they
see as being open to them, concerns the way they
perceive their role as 'homemakers'. Once again,
although many women I spoke to thought that things
were changing in the home and that increasingly men
were helping with domestic chores, at the same time
both at the Superstore and at Roberts Bros, all the
women I interviewed, who were living with a partner,
agreed that it was they, not their partner, who was
ultimately responsible for keeping the house clean,
ensuring that there was food in, doing the washing
and the bulk of the cooking. Male responsibility
towards the home was seen in terms of decorating,
general do-it-yourself home maintenance and, outside
the home, car maintenance and possibly gardening.
The difference in terms of basic responsibility was
nicely caught by Eileen when she said, 'In our house
we do share things, he _helps_ out with the housework
and I _help_ out with the decorating' (emphasis
added). Anne, a shelf-filler at the Superstore who
works four nights a week, revealed the same kind of
underlying assumption as regards the basic responsibility for household tasks when I asked her who did
the domestic chores in her house:

> We share half and half. I always get as much
> done as I can during the day; but when Bob
> comes home he always washes up after dinner
> every night, doesn't matter what night of the
> week it is, and puts the children to bed. But
> then it's the same the other way: I go out to

help with the gardening and painting.

A husband's <u>help</u> with the housework tends not to be
taken for granted: 'I'm very lucky with my husband
because he will help do housework,' (EILEEN). 'Well
of course I have a marvellous husband who helps out
a lot with household tasks,' (LAURA). But however
'good' a husband is, all the women I spoke to shared
the feeling that, whatever else she might choose to
do, it is inbuilt in every woman to be a homemaker
and the responsibility for ensuring that the home
runs smoothly rests with the wife not the husband.
This notion of the basic homemaking propensity of
the female was described expressively by Ella:

> There are men who tell you that they are living
> on their own and that they can cook and they
> can manage, but some of them are not very tidy
> because they don't take that as an interest.
> They couldn't care if the chair is up by the
> bed or if the bed is down by the door as long
> as they get in and get their meal and go to the
> pub. Whereas if a woman is there she will find
> the dust in the window and she didn't touch it
> yesterday, or she finds well I didn't scrub
> that pot last night, I was so tired it was so
> late. Tonight I will make an effort and I'll
> scrub that pot and clean it up and put it away;
> or there are some bits and pieces hanging
> around the house, and I think: I'm off tomorrow
> I'll tidy them up.

Any decisions a woman makes about whether or not to
work, what kind of job she should get, how long
hours she should work and so on, normally, therefore, have as their background an acceptance that
whatever demands the job makes it must be possible
to continue to manage the home. In other words
there are certain commitments which are sacred and
any job which prevents them being fulfilled is
making unreasonable demands. But what about men?
Surely they too have certain commitments to home and
family which it is unreasonable to expect them to
sacrifice to the demands of their job?
  Perhaps the best way of looking at this is to
see the interface between work and home as embedded
in a whole area of ideological norms that define
what are the 'proper', 'reasonable', 'natural',
etc., obligations incumbent upon being an employee,
a mother, a wife, a father, a husband, a daughter, a
son, and all the other myriad of social roles

through which the specific individuality of every individual is always mediated. The negotiation of this sea of conflicting norms, both from the point of view of individuals in the course of their daily life, and in terms of the emergence of commonly shared ideological structures, takes the form of a continual struggle over what the implications of the general norms actually mean in specific concrete circumstances. Is it reasonable for Mrs Jones' employer to refuse her the possibility of promotion because she has young children and can only work a limited amount of overtime? Is it reasonable for Mr. White's firm to demand that he uproot his family and move from one side of the country to the other? Struggle over this clutch of norms is nothing new; the taken-for-granted assumptions of the present day as to the 'proper' balance between work and home are themselves the outcomes of past struggles. None the less, the last few years have seen an opening up of the whole area of work/home relationships to radical and rather new kind of questioning. Fundamental changes in the labour process, the emergence of a new kind of structural unemployment, the resurgence of the women's movement have all played a part in bringing new questioning and whatever the outcome, given the fact that these things are not going to go away, whether people like it or not, 'something is happening'. The old patterns even if as yet not changing radically, seem ideologically at least to be losing something of their unquestioned and taken-for-granted status.

Although this questioning may take the form of an articulated and explicit argument, such as this report, this is not the only form it can take; the very way people live their lives can constitute a questioning. The fact that Mrs Jones does not see why she should be denied promotion, the fact that Mr White argues about his transfer because of the effect it will have on his family is in itself a very concrete form of questioning. The point here is that it is quite possible for people, at one and the same time to express a firm belief in a general norm while, without any hypocrisy, undermining that very same norm by their actions.

But to return to the effect that women's acceptance of their role as homemakers has on their work lives. While this whole area may be undergoing fundamental shifts in attitude, and indeed one of the aims of this report is to contribute to this very debate, none the less, as far as the women at the Superstore and Roberts Bros are concerned, it remains true that quite apart from the question of childcare, the maternal ethic, there is a widely shared sense of responsibility for maintaining the home and keeping it running smoothly.

KATE   It is still very much your responsibility getting the housework done?
KAY   Yes, I still have to rush home.   I left it tidy when I went out this morning, but I know when I get in it's fairly chaotic; toys all over the place, there's dirty baby clothes on the one side and my husband's dirty clothes over here.   I like somewhere to look tidy.   I am not a houseproud mother or housewife, but I like it to look clean and tidy.   So I have to rush home and do that and then bath the baby,   and then feed the baby and play with the baby for a while and get her ready for bed.   Then I usually get dinner ready unless he has got dinner ready for me.   Then it is just a matter of washing up after.   What we generally do is if I cook dinner he is supposed to wash up but he always makes the deal that he will do it in the morning.

Different individuals may have different standards concerning what constitutes a well-run home, but each individual has her own minimum level, and failure to maintain this level results in a feeling of guilt.   For women who have jobs such guilt feelings are likely to involve at some level ambivalence about whether she ought to be working at all.   However conscientious and houseproud a man may be,   he is not liable to this kind of guilt because, as I have already stressed, men are expected to have a job,   Oakley makes the point (1982:150)., that whereas there are endless surveys as to why women work,   men are not asked why they work.   Being a homemaker and being a mother are,   however, expected to cause conflicts for women;   there is an implicit question which all women who have jobs,   or who are considering getting a job, are expected to ask themselves,   namely: does my job, or will my job, interfere with my duties to my family? And if the answer is 'yes' then the solution that is laid down by the prevailing ideology, and which is lodged deep within most women,   is that home and family should come first.

I really couldn't take full-time work now.   I couldn't take the strain of worrying about the work and worrying about the home... what to get for dinner; cleaning up; getting the baby ready for bed... it would be too much. (KAY)

A woman who is married and running a home... her capacity for taking on management level type of work... possibly the pressure of that would be too great. A man if he is married can still continue to do so because he hasn't got to worry about the running of the home thinking about "What are we going to have for dinner?". His main ambition is to earn the money to pay the bills. (FLORENCE)

There is also a difference in the kind of domestic tasks that women and men are responsible for: male tasks tend to be one-off periodic tasks, redecorating a room for instance, which can be fitted in when and as time off work is available. The characteristically female tasks of cleaning, cooking, shopping and so on, in contrast, tend to be those repetitive, essential tasks which have to be fitted into some sort of daily, or near daily routine.

The way women perceive their obligations to their families, both as homemakers and as mothers, and the implicit assumption that there is likely to be a conflict between these and paid employment, leads many women to look for jobs which do not involve responsibility and which do not spill over into their lives outside work. Seventeen of the Superstore women I interviewed were living with a partner and of these twelve gave as one of the reasons why they were working at the Superstore the fact that it was not a demanding job and there was no problem about switching off when they went home. Eileen, Penny and Pat for instance told me:

I don't think I would have liked to go back to doing office work (i.e. when she started working again after having her children)... I used to worry about the work and I used to get headaches and to have a little job where you don't have to worry is nice. I just come home and forget about it. (EILEEN)

PENNY I should think that 75 percent of the women down there (at the Superstore) are married and want to do a job which doesn't hold any responsibility and which they can go and do and then come home and forget about.
KATE Do you feel like that?
PENNY Yes I do, which is why I'm there... I don't say if you've made some terrible bloomer you

completely forget about it, but when you come home you can leave it at work which I think most of the women who work there would prefer to do rather than take any worries home with them. If you're in the managerial sort of thing you take your work home with you don't you? Most of the women if they're married with families just haven't got the time to do so... From my point of view I wanted a job that I could go and do it and leave it there and then go back the next day.

> I like shelf filling it doesn't tax your mind too much - you go in in the evening when you're not at your best when you've been working all day (Pat has two small children) and so often you can just lose yourself in it and get carried away with what you're doing and you might think "what shall I do for dinner tomorrow" because it is easy once you get the hang of it. (PAT)

Given that a woman accepts the particular responsibilities that society allots to wives and mothers, how does this shape her work history outside the home? It is this question to which the next section is addressed.

CAREER ASPIRATIONS AND WORK HISTORIES

Most of the women I interviewed had children; only six of those who worked at the Superstore and five of those who worked at Roberts Bros did not. There was only one woman who did not see herself as having children at some time, 'I just can't see myself having a child. I know it sounds very strange' (FRANCES). Another woman, who was not one of those interviewed, summed up something of the problems of identity involved in any rejection of motherhood and the maternal ethic when she said, explaining her desire for a career, 'I suppose I'm rather a masculine woman.' To reject motherhood is, according to some of the most deeply internalised norms, to deny the essence of being a woman. At the same time motherhood and a full-time job are seen by most women as incompatible at least while the children are young. Of the women I interviewed none of those who worked full-time had pre-school-age children. In an important sense motherhood and the maternal ethic structure the kind of jobs that women do and the sort of work histories they have.

There· are two dimensions involved here: the
objective realities of the sorts of jobs that are
open to women, the kind of childcare facilities that
exist and generally all those objective conditions
which are outside the control of any individual
woman; and then there is also the other whole dimension of the internalised norms and beliefs, all
those powerful 'oughts' which also play a role in
shaping the way people perceive the choices that are
available to them.

## Women's Work

The position of women in the labour market is well
summed up in the following quotation:

> Women's employment has tended to be concen-
> trated in a small number of industries and
> confined to a range of jobs which might be
> described as "women's work". Even where women
> work alongside men, they usually hold positions
> of lower responsibility and perform tasks of a
> less skilled nature... men are the employers,
> managers, top professionals, foremen and
> skilled workers in our society (Oakley,
> 1982:150).

Chart 1.1 (see p.19) shows very clearly the
kind of sexual division of labour which exists. A
few statistics show the kind of realities which lie
behind the 'choices' women make about working.
Most of the low-paid are women. The TUC measure of low pay is 'less than two-thirds of national
average earnings'. In 1982, 50 percent of women
working full-time earned less than this. 10 percent
of men earned less than this. The average weekly pay
of full-time women was 66 percent of men's. The
average hourly pay of full-time women was 74 percent
of men's. (Working Women TUC, 1983:22)
Among other things what this means is that, for
the vast majority of women, it is unrealistic to
aspire to a 'male' income; for most women the
'normal', 'natural' pattern of a woman's life is to
attach herself, usually through marriage, to the
superior earning power of a man. Quite apart from
any other considerations, in straightforward economic terms for most women who want children to
actively choose to be a single parent means to
choose to live in poverty. There is, of course, a
small minority of women who can command 'male'
salaries; on the whole these are women who have

achieved professional or managerial status; they are
women who do a 'man's' job. A small but significant
aspect of this is the way they are often expected to
dress; the smart business suit which is simply an
adaption of the male business suit, and which in its
female guise is meant to play down a too 'feminine'
appearance. The point I am making is that there is
a basic categorisation of certain jobs as appropriate for men and others as appropriate for women;
the fact that some women, normally as a result of
having gained various qualifications on paper, have
managed to break through into the greener pastures
of male employment does not invalidate the fact that
there is this basic categorisation along sexual
lines. It remains true that for the large majority
of women who leave school at sixteen without any
qualifications their real choice is limited to a
range of generally unskilled, low-paid jobs such as
shop work or factory work; and this is before they
have any family commitments. It is not surprising,
therefore, that all the women I interviewed who were
married saw their job as secondary to that of their
husband's. A typical comment was, 'His (her husband's) job is more important to us than mine is...
if he was out of work we'd be right up the... '
(MARJORIE).

Once children come along the possibilities in
terms of employment contract even further. There
was almost unanimous agreement among the women I
interviewed that, except in the case of absolute
financial necessity, they would not contemplate
using any kind of childcare facilities other than
help provided by close relatives. The moral impera-
tive that it is mothers who ought to look after
their children is very powerful. Jo, who herself
earnt a little money by taking another woman's child
to school in the morning, then picking him up in the
afternoon and looking after him until his mother
collected him up at six o'clock, was highly critical
of her charge's mother. 'When she asked me if I'd
have him I said yes, but to me its all wrong... it's
wrong to leave them.' Another woman, who worked
nights after her first child was born, her husband
looking after the baby while she was at work, still
felt very guilty about having worked, saying when I
asked if she would have considered continuing working at that time if there had been suitable childcare facilities:

No, not when they were younger. I felt very
guilty of having to go back to work when my son

was a baby. That was for financial reasons we had to do it. Well, we didn't have to but we would have been stuck in that flat for a long time. I felt very guilty about that, I still do I suppose, I always will. I think when your children are very young you should be there with them, that's why you have them. (PAT)

The one woman at the Superstore who had used a childminder in the past had not had a very happy experience:

My neighbour next door offered to look after him and I thought she'll be alright, she's got three children of her own, but as it turned out it wasn't. He was taken ill and he had gastro-enteritis and was taken to hospital and it was due to him walking around with a dirty bottle in his mouth all the time which this woman had been letting him do... Luckily he pulled through and then from the age of about two until he went to school I packed up work... so after him being ill I felt it was my duty to be at home - it wasn't right to shove him off onto someone else after he'd been ill. So I stayed at home. (DOREEN)

It could be argued that since so many women - my small sample is probably not unrepresentative - seem to reject the very idea of using any kind of child-care facilities, why provide them? There are two important points that should be made here, firstly that however much they may dislike the idea, many women with children have no option but to go out to work and have to make use of some kind of childcare facilities. Single parents who do not wish to rely on payments from the state are an obvious case in point but even those mothers who live with a partner are often, as in the case of the woman quoted above, forced for financial reasons to go out to work. Quite often this need or desire for two incomes is seen as somehow wrong and may be put down to greed:

I think most women are out at work. I don't think people can afford not to work, things are so expensive; but I really think we are getting greedier. We all want bigger houses, like we did and you have to work to get along. (ANNE)

But in fact there is no reason why such aspirations should not be seen as a legitimate desire for a better standard of living.

The second point that should be made is that when women talk about childcare facilities they are thinking of those which currently exist, which as far as Peacehaven is concerned means essentially a choice between a fairly expensive private nursery or a childminder. The fact that people say that they would not use such facilities tells us little about what would happen if free or easily affordable, good childcare facilities were available. While there was a general consensus that mothers with small children should stay at home, two of the women (Jo and Frances) liked the idea of workplace creches. Jo started talking quite spontaneously about work-place creches, having earlier in the interview been quite adamant that mothers ought not to leave their children (see p.44).

> ... there's lots of women who want to work who can't afford to put their kids into play school or find someone to look after them; I think they should have some kind of creche, you know where you go to work. If they had a creche, I mean if you paid 50p a day for somebody just to be in there and look after them. If you had the right sort of set up it could be someone who works there anyway and if you take a week of looking after the children, I think that would be a good idea. (JO)

Female Jobs and Male Jobs

The kind of career aspirations women have and their actual work histories are the joint product of the realities of the labour market and a whole set of internalised norms as to what is an appropriate job for a woman; each side of this equation reinforcing and helping to recreate the other. It is important to be clear, however, as to how the concept of 'appropriate' operates. When I asked people if they thought men and women tended to have different kinds of capacities so that men are more suited to certain jobs, while there are other jobs to which women are more suited, nobody thought that there was a clear natural division of labour based on innate skills and capacities. Certain jobs - coal-mining and building work were the usual ones mentioned - were seen as unsuitable for women, but the jobs that were ruled out for women tended to be seen as exceptions; in the main it was differences between individuals within the same sex that were seen as important

rather than general differences <u>between</u> the sexes.
There was also a widespread feeling that things were
changing and that sexual segregation of jobs was
diminishing. Pat's response was typical:

KATE Do you think in general men and women
tend to have different capacities, tend to be good
at different jobs?
PAT In some jobs, yes, a man might be able to
manage it better, but then you can't always say - it
depends on the personality of the individual. I
don't know about a woman in charge of a building
site full of men, that I don't know... It's like the
roles change over - the mums going out to work and
the dads staying at home. It's surprising the
amount of fathers you see at playschool picking up
their children and at school, and they can cope just
as well... It just depends on the individual.

And yet, at the same time, when it came to the
Superstore women's own career aspirations, with the
exception of Sharon whose lorry driving ambitions I
have already mentioned, they were all highly traditional female jobs. Some of these aspirations were
expressed by young girls who still had hopes of
fulfilling their ambitions, others were the still
remembered dreams of older women; none of the women
with children I interviewed, no matter how young
they themselves were, envisaged themselves as embar-
king on any new career or resuming an old one once
their children were grown up.
Whatever the actual possibilities of resuming
some sort of career, there can be a very real problem of lack of confidence for women who have not
worked for some time. As Jo said:

A lot of women I know who have had kids, have
lost all their confidence because, well, they
have been out of the scene with things going on
and that, they have lost all their
confidence... when you've had a child it
changes you and... I've noticed a lot of my
friends have completely changed after they've
had their children, become a different sort of
person... haven't got as much confidence in
themselves ... They lose touch with everything
and then when they start again they've lost
that confidence. That's all it is really.

Four of the Superstore women I interviewed said
they had never had any particular career ambitions;

the stated ambitions of the rest, some of whom for a time at least had worked in their chosen career, are summarised below:

| | |
|---|---|
| Hairdressing | 4 |
| Beautician | 1 |
| Teaching Dressmaking | 1 |
| Nursery Teaching | 1 |
| Community Care | 2 |
| Nursing | 3 |
| Catering | 3 |
| Clerical | 3 |
| Actress | 1 |

If we add in the various other jobs that the Superstore women had done in the course of their work history to the list of career aspirations, the list gets a little longer, but all the jobs are still ones traditionally associated with women, namely factory work, cleaning and domestic work, shop work, plus one woman who had been in the WRAF.

There tends to be a difference, therefore, between the kind of job options that are seen as available to women in general, and the kind of jobs which are seen by individuals as appropriate to them personally. For example, Frances explained how she personally would never want to do construction, painting or carpentry type work, 'I wouldn't want to do it, it doesn't interest me... I don't know if it's because I'm a woman or what. But that doesn't do a thing. I think if a woman wanted to do it sure, she could do it.' However much people may think that there is a fundamental shift taking place in terms of the kinds of jobs men and women do, as far as the women at the Superstore are concerned these notions do not seem to carry over into the way individuals perceive and live their lives. It is not simply that the job market condemns most women to the ghetto of 'women's jobs' - although this important reality should never be forgotten - but that even in their wildest dreams it seems, most women remain carefully within those territories mapped out as 'suitable for women'.

In the course of my research I also asked local school-children who were approaching school-leaving age about their career aspirations. I asked them to list potential jobs in order of preference. Once again, whatever the children may think about the sexual division of labour in general, when it comes to their own job preferences the girls tended to choose jobs traditionally thought of as appropriate

for women, while the boys opted for traditionally
masculine jobs. The school-children were given a
list of 30 different jobs, mainly non-professional,
and asked to list ten of them. Out of 83 girls none
listed butcher, and just the odd one or two included
warehouse work, builder, labourer or carpenter as
their eighth, ninth or tenth choice; only 24 did not
include hairdresser as one of their choices and 39
included it among their first five choices. Of the
75 boys only eleven included hairdresser among their
choices and only two made it one of their first five
choices. Perhaps the most interesting difference
between the sexes was in regard to the three
categories: working with children, working with old
people and working with animals. The differences
are summarised below:

| | Working with Children | | Working with Old People | | Working with Animals | |
|---|---|---|---|---|---|---|
| Included in First: | 10 | 5 | 10 | 5 | 10 | 5 |
| Girls | 57 | 43 | 35 | 19 | 46 | 25 |
| Boys | 1 | 1 | 2 | 1 | 11 | 6 |

This table provides a very graphic picture of the
way women see themselves, and are seen, as the
'careers' in society.


## BEING A SALES ASSISTANT


## The Division of Labour


i) The BCS Superstore. So far I have sketched out
something of the context within which women execute
their continual balancing act between the two domains of home and work. In this section I want to
look at some of the reality of working in a Superstore and in a department store.
    The composition of the Superstore's workforce
is summarised in Table 2.1 and Chart 2.1. There is
a very clear sexual division of labour. All the
various jobs in the store are graded and each grade
is linked to a particular rate of pay. There are

Women, Work and the Balancing Act

193 employees at the Superstore of whom 169 are
classed either as grade 4 or 5 (the lowest grading
with the lowest rates of pay and covering the till
operators, shelf-fillers, meat packers, sales assistants and trolley boys), eleven are managers or
section heads, four are butchers, three work in the
warehouse, one is a cook in the canteen, while six
work in the office. Managerial and clerical staff
each have their separate grading which is reflected
in the scale of pay. Apart from those six office
workers, all of whom are women, all those above
Grade 4 are men and all are full-time. Until Christmas there was also one woman employed as administrative supervisor for the Grade 4 and 5 workers and
the office workers; but she left and has not been
replaced, instead her responsibilities have been
shared out between two of the office workers and the
checkout supervisor. Women constitute 67 percent of
the total number (193) of employees. Basically each
job in the store can be categorised as characteristically male or female; thus butchers, warehouse
men, trolley boys are male, whereas till operators,
shelf-fillers, meat packers are female. The only
job that is done almost equally by men and women is
that of sales assistant, but even here all the male
sales assistants work in the non-food section
rather than in the food section. There is an important difference, however, between jobs characterised as male and those characterised as female,
for whereas men can, and sometimes actually do female jobs, most of the characteristically male jobs
are barred to women. Thus, although there are no
male till operators at present men are sometimes
employed as till operators, whereas whether formally
or informally, women are barred from Grade 1, 2, or
3, jobs (4). The job descriptions linked to these
grades are set out below:

Grade 1   Butchers' cutters.
Grade 2   Provision hand, wholly or mainly en-
          gaged in boning, cutting and presenta-
          tion of provisions.
Grade 3   Warehouse workers, forklift truck ope-
          rators and porters.

The basic rationale which was given for not
employing women in any of these jobs was always that
they involve heavy lifting, and this was accepted as
reasonable by both men and women and by management
and workers. The fact that some of the men employed
in these supposedly so physically demanding jobs

were extremely weedy 16-year-old lads did not apparently do anything to call this stereotype into
question. The notion that there is an inherent
incompatibility between certain kinds of physically
demanding work and being a woman seems to be deeply
internalised by both men and women. One young
woman, Carol, provided an interesting example of
this. Carol was generally acknowledged by management as being extremely competent with management
potential. She has worked in the store for a number
of years as a basic Grade 5 worker and was asked
fairly recently if she was interested in becoming
manager of the wines and spirits department. The
wines and spirits department is very small and the
position of Wines and Spirits manager is not so
elevated as it might sound. Although Carol is keen
to advance in the store, she turned the job down
because, she later explained to me, 'I want to have
children and I don't want to ruin my insides with
all that lifting.' It is interesting, I think, that
it was not back problems, which after all are the
most likely health hazard involved in lifting, that
Carol fears, but a specific threat to her child-
bearing capabilities.

In the case of management level jobs, lack of
physical strength is a less persuasive argument
against the employment of women; and when talking to
those responsible for hiring at management level or
promoting to management level it was always stressed
to me that there was no bar against women whatsoever. However, at some point in the subsequent
conversation there was nearly always a rider added
to the effect that, yes, of course women have a
right to a career, if that is what they want, but if
they make the choice to have a career then they must
be prepared to accept the responsibility that goes
with it, they cannot expect any concessions because
of their family responsibilities.

I asked May if she thought a woman would be
able to work her way up to management level at the
Superstore:

> If she had the right potential. She'd have to
> work very hard at it. I feel they'd give you
> the chance, but you would have to work that
> much harder. I think you'd need a strong per-
> sonality and someone who wasn't frightened of
> working with management at their own level...
> You'd have to really want to do it and stand no
> nonsense.. you'd really have to work hard.

And this seemed to be the general feeling among the women I talked to. When I asked the same question of Florence, for instance, she said, 'No, providing she was a career woman. She would have to be a career woman.'

Implicit in both the attitude of the management and of the employees is an assumption that whereas some sort of career progression is natural for a man - what needs explaining is if a man does <u>not</u> want promotion - a woman who wants to pursue a career is something of an exception. In reality many men, too, have jobs with few or no prospects of promotion, but what I am concerned with here is the ideology. Women have to prove their management potential in a way that men do not. As Frances put it:

> I read the company magazine and they always have interviews or a part put away in the paper for women who are going into managing or are a successful career type, and it's always how the women have fought and they're proud of where they're at, and how they got there type of thing, whereas I guess with a man it's natural that he would work his way up. With a woman it's an actual job to get up there and prove you can.

Not only do women have to <u>prove</u> they have management potential to their employers, they also have to prove it to themselves, and as I have argued, being a 'career woman' tends to mean to many women to reject the properly feminine family centred role. In line with the ideological opposition between a career and a family orientation, the very qualities that many employers claim as the criteria for assessing management potential, such as a certain assertiveness, a willingness to take responsibility and exercise authority over others are qualities which in men are seen as positive, but in women are viewed more negatively. Men are masterful, women are bossy - the fact that it sounds so odd to describe a man as bossy is very revealing.

ii) <u>Roberts Bros.</u> Roberts Bros, too, appeared to have a clearly marked sexual division of labour, although the sexual mix among the sales assistants is more balanced than at the Superstore, and a considerable number of the department heads are women. Above this level, however, there are relatively few women. I worked at Roberts Bros for a

month and, since my time was so short, I decided to
concentrate on a single department, and so for the
entire month I worked in the haberdashery department. There are 67 people who work in this department, 52 of whom are women and the rest are men.
There are 27 part-timers of whom two, both youngsters who work just Saturdays, are male. The department head is a man, as is his deputy, but three of
the four section heads are women.

In general the attitudes to women and promotion
of both the sales assistants and the management whom
I spoke to at Roberts Bros were very similar to
those at the Superstore; there was the same stress
that while there was no bar to women being promoted,
in order to be promoted a woman would have to demon-
strate that she really was a 'career woman'.

In terms of the work itself, the world of the
department store is interesting in that it tends to
be seen as something of a female domain, serving the
needs of women. This is not to deny that many
customers in both stores are male, indeed I suspect
when expenditure is over a certain amount, responsibility for the purchase tends to shift from the
woman to her partner, but it remains true that
ideologically the customer is thought of as female
rather than male. In both the Superstore and Roberts
Bros the customer is usually referred to as 'she', a
reflection of the fact that ideologically shopping
is seen as a part of the domestic domain of home
and family, the responsibility of which, except in
the case of major purchases, falls on women rather
than men. The world of haberdashery with its ribbons
and lace, its zips, sewing cottons and all the other
home sewing aids, clearly does, in practice as well
as theory, serve a predominantly female clientele.
However, no one working in the department ever
suggested that this made it an unsuitable job for a
man. While I was working in the department I was
very struck by the different way different kinds of
skill and knowledge are regarded. In my interviews I
was often told that perhaps men are better than
women at selling electrical goods, because they have
the necessary technical knowledge. The haberdashery
department is an immensely busy department which is
organised on a largely self-service basis. Anyone
who is out on the shopfloor, however, is continually
assailed by a stream of enquiries from customers
wanting help with their home sewing problems and
very detailed information about the merchandise.
Being an incompetent sewer myself, I found this very
difficult and felt aware of the degree of knowledge

needed to answer all these enquiries, but while there may be a belief that there is a particular area of characteristically male knowledge concerning technical matters and that this gives men the edge in the selling of electrical goods, there does not seem to be a corresponding belief that the characteristically feminine skills of home sewing give women the edge in a department like haberdashery. No one that I spoke to in the department thought that women would be <u>better</u> at selling haberdashery, although some people <u>did</u> say that maybe some men would not <u>want</u> to work with such feminine merchandise. Ellen, for instance, said:

> Even in this department we are working in now (haberdashery) you've got young men working on cutting-desks cutting ribbons and lace and if they're willing to learn about merchandise they can become as expert at it as anybody else.

As I have already mentioned, there is often an important difference between jobs classified as male and those thought of as female in that whereas women cannot do male jobs, such as those of butcher (4), or warehouse work in the Superstore, there is nothing to stop men doing women's jobs; they just tend not to. For instance, for most of the time I was working at the Superstore all the till operators were women, but there was one young man who sometimes worked on the tills, and there had been others in the past. Boys who worked on the tills, I was told, did not tend to stay there long, they tended to get moved or promoted quite quickly.

## Shopwork

Above all else shopwork is about serving customers. Even when, as in the Superstore, the system is one of self-service the need to provide their customers with what those customers want remains central; and the relationship with the customer is at the heart of what it means to work in a shop. Given the relentless pressure to keep staff costs to a minimum - and this applies to both the Superstore and to Roberts Bros - there is a structural tension built into working in a shop, particularly as a sales assistant, resulting from, on the one hand, the desire to provide each customer with as good a level of service as possible and, on the other hand, the need to process customers through the store as speedily as possible. This tension can make a sales

assistant's life very stressful, precisely because
what could be called the labour process of shopwork
takes the form of relationships with people rather
than with things. The kind of satisfaction such
work offers, as Kay expresses so well, stems from a
sense of being able to create genuinely human relationships. Being unable to do this, because of the
need to process customers quickly, can result in
considerable frustration. In answer to my question
of how much skill she thought was involved in selling
Kay said:

> I think there's an awful lot really. I don't
> think you need training. I don't think, par-
> ticularly, you need 'O' or 'A'levels. I think
> you've got to get to know your customers and
> suss your customers out by looking at them. I
> think you've got to like people. You've got to
> like working in a store. It's no good coming
> to work in a store if you don't like people or
> serving customers as such, or thinking you're
> better than anybody else, because you won't get
> on with people, it's just no good, you should
> be away from the shop floor. I don't think you
> need a lot of skills, it all comes in time.
> I've worked on the shop floor now for five
> years and I class myself as an experienced shop
> assistant... I know what I'm doing. I know
> when a customer comes and she's really grumpy
> to leave her grumpy, but I know some customers
> come in grumpy and you can bring them out of
> it, if they're the sort... you've got to know
> them. You've got to know the person virtually
> by looking at them and you've got to know what
> they can afford. Some things are quite expen-
> sive, and especially if they come in with
> children you know that they are watching their
> pennies, but perhaps a bit embarrassed to say
> they can't afford it. You've somehow got to
> know that you can offer them something diffe-
> rent that's not as expensive as what that is,
> but just as good. I think that also is very
> important. I think also you've got to have a
> lot of patience with customers too. With some
> people you try and explain but it doesn't fall
> into place, so you have to speak slower. Then
> you try and explain it like that and if they
> don't understand you try some other way.

The pressure on shopworkers to work fast is something that the older women I talked to tended to see

as something that has got worse over the years. Rose who had worked a lot in shops over the years talked about how shop hours were much longer in the past. 'But,' she said, 'of course the pace of work was so much slower, today they have got you going full pelt.'

When I asked people why they worked at the Superstore, rather than anywhere else, all the women I interviewed cited its convenience, the fact that it was close to where they lived, that it fitted in with their family commitments as the major reasons. None of them talked about the intrinsic satisfactions of the job itself. Similarly at Roberts Bros, although the women thought that the firm was a good one to work for and gave this as one of the reasons for working there, and although they tended to talk more about enjoying selling, the actual job of being a sales assistant, or working elsewhere in a shop, did not seem particularly highly valued. Nobody, for instance, talked about having had any ambition to work in a shop when they were young. The school children I asked about job preferences were also not very enthusiastic about shopwork; of the 83 girls only 15 listed shop assistant among their first five choices, and for the 75 boys the number was 13. Most people, both at the Superstore and at Roberts Bros, described shop work to me as basically unskilled; and this is a definition that most people perhaps would accept, but what exactly does 'skilled' mean? A question which brings us to the next section.

## SKILL AND TRAINING

### Skill, Experience and Commonsense

The term skill is one of those words which we all tend to use quite happily, confident that its meaning is clear and known to everyone, but once we start to look at it a little more carefully, all its simplicity and straightforwardness begins to evaporate. Skill is in fact a very vague and general concept which is used to describe a whole range of often rather different kinds of aptitudes and knowledge. One distinction that it is important to be clear about in the context of women and employment is the distinction between skill meaning the learnt ability to do something such as drive, sew, deal with difficult customers, and skill used in the context of employment to mean a certain level of

competence and knowledge <u>deserving of</u> a <u>particular</u>
<u>level</u> <u>of</u> <u>remuneration</u>. The point here is that while
there is an enormous variety of human skills in the
sense of capacities and knowledge which are not
inherent, instinctual capacities, but have to be
learnt, only some of these skills are recognised as
being valuable in the labour market. One particular
range of skills which tend to be little valued in
the labour market consists of all those domestic
skills which are usually thought of as especially
feminine, such as the skills of childcare, housework, cooking and so on. Only if they have undergone the transformation brought about by a professional training, as in the case of a chef, do the
skills of the domestic world begin to have a value
in the labour market. Very frequently it seems this
transformation also involves a change of sex; a
woman's place may be in the home and the kitchen may
be her sovereign domain, but the kitchens of the
<u>haute</u> <u>cuisine</u>, where the preparation of food has
become a commodity, are overwhelmingly male.

Being a shop assistant is generally regarded as
an unskilled job, an assessment which is reflected
in the low level of pay. Before looking at the
management side of this and the whole question of
training, I want to explore something of the kind of
perceptions women workers themselves have about
skill and about what it means. The women I interviewed at Roberts Bros were all sales assistants; at
the Superstore they were all Grade 4 or 5 workers
and included people who had worked on the delicatessen section, the butchery, non-foods, the checkouts and people who were shelf-fillers. Apart from
the shelf-fillers who all had small children and who
had chosen that particular job because it had fitted
in with their domestic commitments, which section a
woman worked on at the Superstore seemed to depend
mainly on what job was going when she applied.
Within the Grade 4 and 5 jobs there did not seem to
be any particular status-ranking; certain individuals preferred certain jobs, some liked a lot of
contact with customers, for instance, others did
not, but this was seen purely as a matter of personal preference.

When I asked in the Superstore how much skill
they thought their job and shop work generally
involved, the general response was to begin, at any
rate, by denying that there is much skill involved.
May, Dawn and Jo, for instance, began their answers
as follows:

MAY Not anything (this was in relation to the packing of meat).
DAWN I don't think anyone needs any particular skill.
DOREEN I wouldn't say it was a skill, I'd just say it's common sense really; not a skill.

May went on to compare the packers' lack of skill with the skills of the male butchers saying, 'There's no comparison, not with what the butchers do; no.' She then described what the packers job involves:

MAY You have to learn the cuts (of meat) and the machine (which weighs the meat and prints the price tickets), but given six months you should know by looking at meat what it is; it's not a skill. You've just got to think. It's the machines; the weights and measures are so important, so you must use the right tare (the paper trays on which the meat is placed before it is wrapped in plastic film) and check your machine. It's like wrapping, it takes a while. After three and a half years (the length of time May has worked at the store) you can do it very fast. When you first go in there you're all fingers and thumbs and you think "Oh, my god". The first thing I had to wrap was a chicken. If you'd seen it, its legs were sticking out and I never thought I'd ever be able to do it, but within four days of trying I could do it and then your speed comes. It's not skilled at all; it's all common sense a lot of it. Dealing with the public that's where you have to learn.
KATE How long did it take you to get up a decent speed wrapping?
MAY I didn't take too long... I should think to get really settled in a couple of months... but it took three to four months looking at meat to learn the different cuts of meat... If you use your common sense and you're there for about three months, you should be able to do it reasonably well.

I have already quoted Kay's account of the kind of skill in dealing with people working in a shop entails (p.55) and many of the women, although they might not define this as a real skill, focussed on dealing with customers as the most demanding part of their job. Penny at the Superstore put it like this:
I think the main skill is dealing with the public as against the actual job itself. Most

of it is common sense. You have to know how to talk · to people - people with bad tempers if they've been waiting a long time, this sort of thing.

Skill or common sense? Ellen, who works at Roberts Bros, also felt that the qualities her job demanded were not exactly skills:

KATE How much skill do you think there is involved in selling?
ELLEN In a place like this? To my mind there are some people who can deal with the general public in any situation and some who can't... if you're someone who doesn't know how to deal with the public it's not really a skill you can learn. <u>It's not a skilled job in the sense that you need qualifications</u>... but there is a sort of skill, I suppose, in that if you want to do it well you have got to know about what you are selling, you've got to know how to handle yourself and the general public. You've got to be an outgoing kind of personality so you can put yourself across. <u>Whether you call that a skill or not... it's not something you go and train for.</u> A place like this (Roberts Bros) provides training... it helps you. You can go on courses about how to deal with difficult customers, customers' complaints and all different situations where you can learn how to cope; but if you've got any sort of sense and you're aware of things then you are going to learn by your own mistakes as you go along... <u>there is a sort of skill but not the sort you go to a college or specific place to train for.</u> Lets face it there's very little brain work involved as such, mental work.

Skill here is being defined essentially in terms of formal paper qualifications. Anything else is seen as either a question of natural, inherent aptitude, or as simply the result of experience. The importance of this, as far as the labour market is concerned, is that neither natural aptitude, unless it is a very exceptional and unusual talent such as for music or acting, nor experience that is not linked to more formal qualifications, are highly regarded and tend to be poorly rewarded financially. Also as far as career prospects are concerned they tend to count for little. As Kay put it:

I think basically as far as degrees and that go you don't really need them for that (selling),

but if you're going to go on, perhaps get on
with a career, nowadays you do need 'O' and 'A'
levels and degrees in this and that. I wanted
promotion after a while and I found it extremely tough for me to get promotion because there
were so many graduates coming in... I wouldn't
say they were particularly intelligent... in
fact they didn't know how to serve or sell.
All they were good at was being super efficient
with paperwork, well that isn't any good on the
shop floor. I think that it is totally unfair
and I still do. They know the ones who work
and when you get a graduate who perhaps has got
a degree in History, because she's got that
degree in History or Art that makes all the
difference and I don't see why it should, I
think that is really unfair, I think they
should go by experience.

To paraphrase what Kay is saying: what seems to
matter is who you are, not how you perform.
   In retailing, as in so many other industries,
there is and has been for a long time, a process of
de-skilling taking place. In the case of manufacturing, de-skilling characteristically takes the
form of splitting the labour process into smaller
and smaller units so that each individual worker
becomes responsible for a smaller and smaller part
of the whole process; in the retail trade, however,
although the way goods are processed through the
system can be broken down in this way, that vital
part of the labour process which involves the relationship with real live customers has as its essence
a qualitative, human dimension resistant to any
reduction to the purely quantitative. Kay describes
the hectic pace of the haberdashery department
cutting-desk (where the ribbons, lace, elastic, etc.
that are sold by the metre are cut to customers'
requirements) in the following way, 'You haven't got
time to talk to the person on your right or your
left. You've got to talk to the customer, move them
on and get another one in.'
   Even at the checkouts of the Superstore a certain human relationship is valued by both customers
and till operators. Peacehaven, being a relatively
small community and the Superstore having something
of a monopoly, at times the store can have quite a
village shop atmosphere. Some of the older cashiers
in particular are able to maintain a very chatty,
friendly relationship with their customers while at
the same time sacrificing none of their speed in

checking through what has been bought. But this kind of skill, although productive in the sense of being valued by customers as making the Superstore more pleasant to shop in, is not seen by either management or staff as a real skill; apart from the need to develop a certain manual dexterity, the job of cashier is seen as one demanding no particular skill at all.

At Roberts Bros, where there is the rather different legacy of the old-time department store, some of the older sales assistants talked to me about how different things were in the past when, as they saw it, being a sales assistant in a store like Roberts Bros was a genuinely skilled job. What has brought about this sense of a loss of skill is not that there has been a de-skilling (in that their labour process has been divided up with each individual only carrying out a part where they used to carry out the whole) - although it is true there has been a tendency for stock control to become increasingly centralised. What has happened is that the significance of the sales assistant/customer relationship has diminished as the pressure to increase the volume of sales, while not increasing - preferably cutting down on - the labour force, has grown ever more insistent. The resulting impoverishment of the quality of shop workers' lives can be considerable. The importance of the relationship with customers for many shop workers, even when the service element in their job seemed to have been cut to the bone, is indicated by the way so many of the women at the Superstore, whether they worked in the tills, the delicatessen counter or on any of the other sections, would often talk about their particular customers who would only come through their till, or would insist on being served by them.

Training
The BCS' and Roberts Bros' approaches to training are very different. The BCS employs one full-time training officer for its 1,800 employees; at Roberts Bros, who employ over 2,000 staff, there is a training department with ten people, of whom nine are full-time. At the Superstore training primarily takes the form of training on the job: when a newcomer begins work, they are put with a more experienced worker who is expected to teach the newcomer their job. Although this works quite well provided the person doing the training is conscientious and happens to be a good teacher, newcomers,

61

Women, Work and the Balancing Act

particularly if they are a bit shy, can be left feeling rather lost. Pat, for instance, remembered her first evenings as a shelf-filler as a bit difficult:

KATE When you first started what sort of training did you get?
PAT On my first night I went round with J... and she was showing me and telling me what to do . And the next night... I didn't realise most people went to a particular aisle.. so I tended to float around and I upset a couple of girls once because I'd got the soap powder list and I was doing that and they came up to me and said, "WE always do this." I thought, "Oh, crumbs," so I went somewhere else and in the end I asked one of the girls what the routine is... and she said, "I'm always down on cereals, M. is on holiday this week so come down there with me." (and Pat has stayed on the cereal aisle ever since).

On the tills newcomers, even those who have never operated a till before, are put straightaway with one of the old hands who trains them at the same time customers are being served. Once again the training period is brief:

KATE What sort of training did you have?
FLORENCE Very little. I started on a Tuesday and it was very busy. Dot gave me my training. I was with Dot and Dot showed me all the different departments (each purchase section: butchery, grocery, or whatever, has to be recorded on the till). I suppose because I'm very adaptable I picked it up very quickly. After about half an hour she had me sitting on the till and after two hours I was ready.

Things are much the same on the delicatessen section:

KATE What about the training you got at the Superstore?
FRANCES Two hours... well to be fair that's the type of job where you can't be trained... So when I was there... for about three hours I just followed Julia and I watched her and I was on my own. If I had problems I asked and was shown.

As one might expect, on every section what in fact happens is that the managers tend to rely on a

62

few of the longer serving employees and the same few
people always get asked to show the newcomer the
ropes. Those who carry out this training are not
given any extra payment, even on the tills where the
trainee uses the trainer's till, and it is the
latter who is responsible for any mistakes. This
causes a certain amount of resentment:

JO I've been there four years and a lot of the
time they say "Can you take this new girl and show
her what to do." But that's all wrong because once
they're with you on that floor that's it. They
never come up to make sure you're doing everything
right and we are training them and I think we should
get training money... But you don't; you're used to
train the girls when it's not up to me, it's their
job.

The management of the Superstore is made up of
people who have worked their way up from the shop
floor, and when I talked to them about the question
of training they usually expressed a certain
cynicism as to the value of any kind of formal
training. Even the Co-operative movement's own
college at Loughborough, where some of the Superstore's employees go for short courses, was sometimes seen as academic and out of touch with the
reality of actual stores. There was certainly no
question here of experience not being sufficiently
valued, but unfortunately for the Grade 4 and 5
women employees only certain kinds of experience
seem to count. The managers saw their own management skills as the product of experience, but they
were very dismissive when I tried to suggest that
even if the women they employed did not have formal
skills such as paper qualifications, perhaps a
number of them nevertheless had, as a result of
their experience in other jobs or simply their
experience of managing a home and family, considerable skills particularly as far as dealing with
customers was concerned.
The employees at the Superstore do have some
formal training. At some time in their first six
months each full-time employee is supposed to attend
a day's induction session in which they are told
about the history of the BCS and the Co-operative
movement generally. What there does not seem to be
is any training in the actual business of selling
and dealing with customers. As May put it, thinking
not so much of herself but of some of the youngsters
straight from school who often find dealing with

customers something of a problem, 'They've told us they want people to be polite to customers so they don't have complaints, but they don't tell them how.'

There are also the various short courses run by the Co-operative College at Loughborough, and a few other courses run by the one BCS training officer. In general, however, it is true to say that there is very little training within the BCS for non-management staff, so that even if a woman is interested in promotion there is no real training programme she can use as a ladder to advance through the organisation.

At Roberts Bros there is a much greater stress on training, although in terms of acquiring the basic skills of being a sales assistant once again these are learnt primarily 'on the job'. When a new person starts, their first morning is spent listening to a short talk explaining the store and the way it is run, and being shown round the store. Also, once a week the store opens half an hour later in order to allow a half hour training period, although in fact, as I explain below, this half hour should more accurately perhaps be called an information half hour.

In contrast to the women I talked with at the Superstore, most of the women - or at least the full-timers of Roberts Bros - have participated in a number of training courses. Dawn, who has been working as a sales assistant at Roberts Bros for about a year, before which she worked for about three and a half years in the hairdressing department, was enthusiastic:

DAWN  I think the training schemes here are very good. I've had a lot of training from Roberts Bros... I've been to all the courses here and courses away and they've all been paid for. I've never had to pay for anything. I think it's really good.

KATE  Those courses, were they while you were doing hairdressing or since you've been on the shop floor?

DAWN  A lot while I was hairdressing. I was sent to Liverpool and stayed in a five-star hotel for a weekend. That was a cutting course. Then I went to the L'Oreal School in London for a colouring course... I think I've been really lucky.

KATE  What sort of courses have you done while you've been on the shop floor?

DAWN  Mainly sort of video, talking into a

video (5), Roberts Bros, general selling, introductory courses. About four or five I've been on, different ones.
KATE Have they been useful to you?
DAWN Oh, yes.

At the same time, however, the various courses she had attended had not changed Dawn's belief, quoted on p.58, that sales assistants don't need any particular skill. Kay had been on a number of courses when she was working full-time; although she had enjoyed her courses on the whole, when I asked how much she thought they had helped her in terms of her work on the shop-floor she said, 'None of it really.' Of course the fact that someone does not perceive that their training has improved their work performance does not necessarily mean that it really has had no effect; if someone is firmly convinced, for instance, that shopwork does not entail what they regard as real skills they are likely to underestimate the role of training.

Leaving aside that question, the role of training may not only involve a straightforward imparting of skills and knowledge, it may also be about strengthening the individual's sense of belonging to a particular organisation, and their sense of being recognised and valued as a person in their own right. There was certainly a marked contrast between the Superstore's employees' attitudes to management and those of the Roberts Bros employees, which brings us to wider questions than simply training and deserves a new section.


COMMUNICATION AND POWER

Nearly all the women I interviewed at the Superstore complained to me about the way they were treated by the managers and the managers' attitude in general. The shelf-fillers were particularly unhappy:

KATE How do you find the attitude of the managers at the Co-op generally?
PAT Not very nice... I was surprised when I got there - the way they speak to you as if you've got no sense or no brains really, even at school I wasn't spoken to like that.
DIANE I think at the Co-op you're treated so much... I don't like the attitude they have there, it's as if they don't trust you an inch... They treat the staff... it's like being back at school.

You're treated with no more respect than a school-child. I think particularly as a lot of the management are young. Some of the women have a lot more experience - they shouldn't be treated like that.
    MARJORIE I've just had enough of the way they (the managers) treat you....I mean we are grown married women with children and responsibilities and yet they think we've got the mentality of a three-year-old. We can't use our own initiative; we've got no inititiatve of our own. We can't do anything unless they tell us what to do and I think all the girls have got the same opinion.

But these kind of feelings were not limited to the shelf-fillers. Doreen, who worked on the non-foods section was also very critical of certain of the management, particularly those on the food side.

    DOREEN It's gone to their heads, they think that because they are managers they have the right to be rude to whoever they want and that seems to be the only way they can get over to anyone.
    KATE Do you think their attitude has got something to do with why some people don't like working at the Co-op?
    DOREEN I do definitely. To an extent you should still speak to people in a way you'd expect to be spoken to. Regardless of whether you are a manager or a shelf-filler, you're still human. You're working under the same roof and it would make life easier if they respected each other.

Time and time again, not only in my interviews, but spontaneously when people were sitting chatting over coffee in the canteen or simply exchanging a joke while they were working, the same bitter resentment of what was seen as a denial of their individuality as human beings would surface. Penny expressed it very well:

    PENNY One thing I do object to, when you really have had a very hard day and nobody turns round and says, "Thank you." I don't mean that way, by money in the hand, I do mean just thank you, and I find that very discouraging. It goes an awful long way if somebody just says, "Thank you."
    KATE Do you feel that they could do more about making people feel part of the store?
    PENNY Yes, by just simple courtesy. Saying, "Good Morning" and saying, "Thank you" if you have had an Easter or Christmas, when you really do work

extremely hard. If someone came out to the counter just as you were leaving and said, "Thanks very much, you've all done very well" etc, it would make you feel ten times better than just looking at you and saying, "Are you still here?" sort of attitude, "Why haven't you gone home?"

Another element in this general resentment linked to the lack of acknowledgement by management was the feeling that the management did not keep the staff sufficiently informed about management decisions concerning the running of the store, the reasons for those decisions and so on. Rose would frequently complain to me, "They never tell us anything up there, that's what makes me so cross." Certainly my experience of working in the Superstore was that when a new rule, for instance, was brought into force, employees would be simply told that this new rule existed with no attempt to explain why it had been introduced. When I first went to the Superstore I was struck by the fact that there was no regular time set aside when management could get together with staff and discuss any problems that had come up, or could explain any changes that were being made. This was in marked contrast to Roberts Bros' weekly half-hour training. Florence talked about this lack:

> I do feel that there should be staff meetings every so often where you can air your grievances to management and management can air their grievances to you, any problems you're finding with regards to your working conditions, as a place where you can air them out. But you do not get this opportunity... There are a lot of youngsters up there who don't even know who (the Store Manager and the Deputy Manager) are. Alright, maybe they're not supposed to know, but it's nice for the heads of the Co-op to know that people know them.

As I have already mentioned, the training half hour at Roberts Bros is more accurately described as an information half hour. Each department has its own separate meeting, presided over by the head of the department, for example, while I was working there, the haberdashery department had a speaker from a firm that manufactures sewing threads, and a visit from one of Roberts Bros' own personnel officers. Sometimes a member of the department gives a talk; Ellen, for instance, one of whose hobbies is lace-making, had given a talk on lace. As well as these talks, the sales figures for the department are discussed and the previous week's or fortnight's figures are compared with the figures for the same weeks in the previous year. Staff are also shown new merchandise, and the manager has an opportunity to talk about any topic he or she thinks relevant. The rest of the staff are free to ask any questions they want, but from what I observed it is more a case of the manager answering specific questions the staff may have about topics he has raised rather than an opportunity for the staff to provide a real input of information into management. At the same time, however, all the staff of the haberdashery department that I talked to, liked this half hour; they seemed to enjoy the talks on the whole and were appreciative of the fact that the manager took the time and the trouble to explain what was happening in the department, and to give them some feedback, in terms of the sales figures, on what their selling efforts were achieving. As well as this communication on the shop floor, Roberts Bros also has a staff council which meets several times a year and is an important forum for discussion between all levels of management; anything may be discussed here from the lengths of coffee breaks to the firm's financial results. The emphasis on communication, generally, at Roberts Bros seems to be very much appreciated by the staff:

> The job (at Roberts Bros) is like a secure job to be in. You feel more safe and secure for the reason you are told lots of things... nothing is hidden, (ELLA).

Something else which was clearly important to people was being recognised as a particular individual rather than being no more than a cog in the machine. As Kay said, 'I'm not a number, I'm a person.'

While it is important not to confuse the sharing of information with the sharing of power, the general stress on communication at Robert Bros apparently does help give employees some sense of individual recognition; a sense which was quite clearly lacking at the Superstore, and may have more than a little to do with their very high rate of labour turnover. In 1983 the turnover of the Grade 4 and 5 staff, and almost all the women the Superstore employs are Grade 4 or 5, was approximately 90 percent. This was seen as rather exceptional, but the BCS expects a yearly turnover of something like 50 percent. At Roberts Bros the labour turnover among non-management staff is below 15 percent.

## TRADE UNIONS

As far as Roberts Bros is concerned, I found little evidence that the sales staff belong to any union, consequently this section deals solely with the Superstore. Like all stores run by Co-operative Societies, the BCS has a post-entry closed shop arrangement with the Union of Shop, Distributive and Allied Workers (USDAW), which means that anyone working at the Superstore has to become a member of USDAW and it is USDAW which negotiates wage rates, conditions of work and so on with the BCS.

With certain honourable exceptions, the trade union movement throughout its history has tended to focus on the needs of male full-time workers. Even today there is a widespread gut feeling among many trade unionists that women, and particularly part-timers, do not make good trade unionists. One of the factors underlying this kind of prejudice, I would argue, is once again the notion that women necessarily and properly think of themselves primarily as wives and mothers rather than as workers. To show how wrong this kind of prejudice can be, it is worth mentioning two different examples of individual women's attitudes to trade unions, and in particular the union at the Superstore.

The first example concerns Jane and illustrates the dramatic way people's attitudes can change in a short space of time. Jane works full-time on the delicatessen counter and is married with two school-age children. Her husband has a reasonably well-paid management level job and they own their own house and run a car. Generally Jane fits the stereotype of the middle-class housewife working to bring in money for 'extras', whose attitudes and beliefs are closer to those of the employer than they are to those of the employee. When I interviewed her she was, as were virtually all the women I interviewed, very dismissive both of the union at the store and unions in general. She had never been to a union meeting, had no intention of ever going to one, and could not see how the union was, or could be, relevant to her. A few weeks later, however, things had changed. Some Superstores run by Co-operative Societies, but not the Peacehaven one, pay slightly higher wage rates because they are Superstores.

Women, Work and the Balancing Act

From the beginning of my fieldwork I heard talk about the Superstore rate, some telling me that the Peacehaven store employees would automatically be paid the Superstore supplement in the near future, and some telling me that there was no such thing as a Superstore rate. Over the months of my fieldwork the question of the Superstore rate became more and more of an issue, with a few individuals arguing that the only way the Peacehaven employees would get the Superstore rate was through the union, and people began to talk about going to the next union meeting. Although the store has a post-entry closed shop, the level of union activity at the store is very low and hardly anyone goes to the union meetings which are held once a month in Brighton. Due largely to the efforts of one of the till operators who organised transport and generally chivied people about, fifteen of the till operators attended the October union meeting and the question of the Superstore was raised. The next day rumours started circulating that there was to be a new Superstore rate but only the till operators were going to get it. Jane and the other women who work on the delicatessen counter, none of whom had been at the meeting, were incensed and a couple of days later I met Jane and her attitude to the union had completely changed. Now she was sure that the only way the store's employees would get the new Superstore rate would be if the union fought for it and she was outraged at the thought that it might just be paid to the till operators. She told me how she and some of the other delicatessen people were determined to go, and indeed come November they duly turned up at the union meeting in Brighton. They were quite vocal at this meeting. Jane herself raised a number of grievances about general working conditions in the store and the particular problems of those working in the delicatessen section.

Although both in the course of the meeting and in talking with her afterwards, Jane expressed some scepticism about the union and its ability to do anything for the store's employees, the union for her had changed from being some remote entity, uninterested and uninteresting, into something , however flawed, which had a real relevance for her. Jane's change in attitude, however, does not mean that she has necessarily changed her attitude to unions in general, and if asked a general question about trade unions in Britain will probably still maintain 'they have too much power' and are 'ruining the country'.

My second example is taken from my interview

70

with Jo, who is married with two small children and works part-time as a shelf-filler, and shows the kind of disjuncture there can be between someone's stated beliefs when elicited in different contexts, and between someone's beliefs and the way they act. The fact that individuals do not behave in accord with their stated beliefs, or contradict themselves, does not necessarily imply that they are lying or insincere; rather it often points to the fact that the way an individual translates a belief or idea into action can never be taken for granted. For all of us the paths between thought and action are frequently convoluted and murky. The following is an extract from quite early in my interview with Jo:

KATE  What do you feel about unions generally?
JO  A load of rubbish. The ruin of the country they are.
KATE  In what way?
JO  They are, aren't they?  If you didn't have all these unions and people going out on strike and that, I mean, a lot of the jobs you see on the telly, oh the union have brought them out on strike like a month later, like they're closing the place down because the union have taken them out on strike, so the work's not getting done, and I mean down there you don't even know that you've got a union.
KATE  I mean do you know who the union representative is?
JO  No.
KATE  It was Henrietta who worked on...
JO  Don't even know her.  I mean, they had a union meeting down there one time and we were told we couldn't go.  It didn't bother me cos I'm not interested in it anyway.

Later on in the interview, however, when we were talking about the managers at the store and how a lot of the women there lacked the confidence to deal with them, Jo started talking about a particular incident at the store:

JO  ...we worked at Christmas time or something and we was told we would get paid for it, but we didn't and they were all moaning about it, but there was nothing they could do about it, so of course I said, "The only way you're gonna get anything done is for all of you to go in there together, it's no good one or two of you going." So about half past seven one night we all just put down our pricing guns and went in the office and said we weren't doing no more work until we got it sorted out. Of course they didn't stand a chance 'cos there's no way they can sack all twenty of you. The next day they're not going to find twenty girls to come in and do the same job, plus they got to train them all up. Of course we got our money. But they just won't do it.

I then suggested that perhaps this was just what unions were all about, to which she responded:

JO ...before, when they were looking for a shop steward they said why don't you go for it and I said because I couldn't be bothered, it wouldn't get you nowhere and all this business and I said I'd probably end up losing my job if I open my mouth too much, and of course I wouldn't do it. I think the night girls should have a person that could speak for them, but they don't.
KATE And you wouldn't be that person?
JO I would if I knew it would be alright, but at the moment I know it wouldn't, you just wouldn't get anywhere.
KATE But perhaps that is what a union is partly about because it gives you that protection.
JO If the union said, "Right, Milly Mophead is going to be the representative for the night girls, and she's got our backing all the way," then somebody would do it, but when you haven't got anything behind you and you know they could say, "She's getting too what's-its-name, we'll get rid of her," 'cos they would, they'd find something to get rid of you, they'd watch you and then the minute you did something wrong that would be it.

The kind of suspicion that certain trade unionists have of part-time women workers is in part simply a reflection of the way such workers tend in general to be regarded. In the next section I want to examine the whole concept of part-time in more detail.


FULL-TIMERS AND PART-TIMERS

Whatever people may feel about the relative merits of part-timers and full-timers, that part-time and full-time are two obviously and easily distinguished categories is agreed by everyone. In any work place there is always a sharp line drawn between those who work full-time and those who work part-time. When I asked Diane (a part-timer) if she thought that the Superstore would benefit from more training, she said:

> I think they would benefit if they had more full-time, proper staff and not so many part-timers. I don't think any of the staff have any responsibility towards their jobs because they're only a few hours here and there.

Frances (a full-timer) was more positive about part-timers:

> Part-time is just as serious as full-time, you are just there for a few hours less... If you are part-time, just the few hours you come in you are going to put more into it than if you were there full-time. Because if I was on that counter part-time, I'm sure I would put more into it than I did when I was full-time (when I interviewed Frances she had just left her job at the Superstore), because after full-time you just... I mean it just wears you out. Because the days I've had when I put in four hours when I took off early, I put more into that four hours than I did into eight hours.

Rose (a part-timer) felt very strongly about the way part-timers are treated. I asked her if she thought part-time workers should be treated the same way as full-time workers:

> Oh definitely, because they're a necessity. I mean why take us on if we're not necessary? So we should be treated the same. I know they're under the impression that when we get there we haven't done anything. They forget they've got out of bed, had their breakfast got for them, some of them, and they go straight to work and then they probably go home and have their meal put on the table for them and they don't do anything else. But we come in: I've got to get the meal in the morning before I come, or I usually have to do some cleaning, or get the meal ready for when I come in. There're always different things to do.

At the same time one of the most commented on trends in patterns of employment common to most modern industrial economies is the increase in the employment of part-timers, particularly women. It is interesting that although in terms of the number of hours worked the definition of part-time varies, and that there may be some ambiguity in the case of specific individuals, it seems to be generally assumed that the distinction between full-time and part-time is simple and straightforward, as is the classification of any workers as full or part-time. Thus no employee at the Superstore or Roberts Bros had any hesitation in telling me whether they worked full or part-time, and as far as the BCS, USDAW and Robert Bros are concerned the cut-off point is clear: part-timers work less than 30 hours per week. Interestingly, employees who work more than 30 hours a week, but less than 39 hours, would invariably describe themselves as part-time. The store management too, although allowing such workers the sick pay, holiday pay and other entitlements of the full-timer, when it came to a question of promotion, or if they were asked in a particular case, if such a worker were full-time or not, would invariably define them as part-time. What we have here, I would argue, is a concept, 'full-time', which although ostensibly concerned with the quantative question of how many hours a person works, is at another level concerned with more qualitative questions as to the kind of worker a particular individual is, and what role their job plays in their life. Behind the two labels, part-time and full-time, there lurks, often at a largely unconscious level, two opposed yet linked sets of characteristics which can be summed up as follows:

| Full-timers | Part-timers |
| --- | --- |
| Breadwinners. | Working for 'pin money', a 'bit extra'. |
| Serious commitment to job. | Lack of serious commitment to job. |
| A full member of the organisation, an insider. | Not a full member of the organisation, an outsider. |
| Reliable. | Unreliable. |

In listing these characteristics I am arguing neither that they are accurate, nor that everybody always has them in mind when they talk about full-time and part-time, I am simply trying to drag out into the light some of the deep beliefs that often colour the way particular categories of workers are seen. An extract from my interview with Sharon illustrates the kind of assumptions which are common. I asked what was the status of one of the women, Julia, who worked on the delicatessen counter vis-a-vis the other women on the counter, to which the reply was:

SHARON She's been there the longest but she's not full-time, she's part-time... she's been there the longest, the managers and all the rest of it... if there is anything to complain about they go and complain to Julia. It gets on my nerves that they do that because in a way I suppose I've got more authority over her because I'm full-time and she's only part-time.

KATE Do you think full-timers always have authority over part-timers?

SHARON Well, yes I suppose so, because full-timers are there all the time and they know what they are doing, where a part-time person is employed and they can be relieved at any time, and they are only meant to be there for a certain amount of time. The full-timers, they are there and they are employed by the actual place as a long time person.

KATE But some of the part-timers at the Co-op... I mean Julia does about 30 hours, so that is quite a lot.

SHARON When you said that I think in some ways Julia can tell us what to do. When I was part-time I felt that if it was somebody who was full-time told us what to do they had got authority. When I became full-time I thought if somebody was part-time and they turned round and told me what to do, they've got no right to tell me because they are only part-time and I'm full-time. I don't know why. But I did. I suppose I just thought that. Don't ask me how.

I think it is clear here that although Sharon tries to relate her basic gut feeling about full-timers and part-timers to the length of time they work, this feeling is more closely related to differential levels of commitment. Penny also talked to me about Julia:

PENNY Julia is one of the examples to me of where you can work and work and never get any further... Julia would be the prime example of being a supervisor, but only because she's part-time she can't be.

KATE Do you think that's fair?

PENNY Well, if you're going to be a supervisor you've got to be there all the time, haven't you?

Dawn at Roberts Bros was quite clear about what she saw as the different levels of commitment of part-timers. I asked her if she thought part-timers should have the same rights and the same opportunities for promotion as full-timers:

DAWN Maybe sick pay and that kind of thing, but with promotion I think it should be given to those people who are prepared to work hard for it and I don't think it would really be fair to them if somebody got promotion who only worked part-time. I think it would cause a lot of havoc between people who do work full-time and work hard and slog their guts out until they are promoted. I think they are fairly well treated here anyway, the part-timers, I think sometimes they probably get a better deal than full-timers.
KATE Do you think in general part-timers tend not to be so committed as full-timers?
DAWN The part-timers here, they work really hard, but probably not... I mean full-timers, if you're going to do that it's more of a career isn't it... people who have had children, you really just want to work a few days and earn some money, well they just enjoy coming in a few days a week. But I think if an opportunity was given to them to have a career I think a lot of them would turn round and probably say no... I think it's right as it is... I know a lot of people who have been managers here have come back... had children and have gone back on the shop floor as rank and file.

I went on to press Dawn a little on this:

KATE And do you think that's fine?
DAWN Yes, I think it must be degrading for them though... I don't think I could do it. We've had people training with us, they've come back and I say to them, "Haven't I seen you somewhere before?" and they say, "Well, actually I was manager of china," or something like that, and you step back in your shoes... I think that's the most horrible part of it .. I mean you do all that training and then you just go away for maybe a year and have a child and then come back... it's fair, it's a fair way of doing it really, I suppose... I don't know... it's the way it goes.

Dawn was beginning not to sound quite so sure after all, and I pressed her a bit more:

KATE You don't think possibly it's a bit wasteful of all that training?

DAWN Oh yes... But I suppose when children come along, I don't know, I mean it's one's personal decision isn't it? I think probably sometimes people do become managers and it's maybe a waste when you do come back and have to go on the floor as rank and file. I hate that word rank and file.

Even though Dawn seems to have shifted her ground a little, she is still seeing the question of waste in terms of individuals choosing to give up their careers, rather than in terms of a system which, because of the way it is currently organised, forces people into choosing between career and family. It is important here that the options involved are not paid employment or family, but career or family. Part of the major ideological significance of the concept of part-time work is that it is work which does not demand, as does the traditional work ethic, that here is where the individual should locate their primary moral responsibility. To reiterate what I said earlier about the male role of bread-winner; within the ideology at least, there is no contradiction between a man's obligations to his job and to his family, because the 'proper' means through which his obligations to his family are met is through his role as breadwinner. Part-time work carries little of the moral baggage of full-time work, it is work that is expected to be fitted round other obligations individuals have.

Kay, who now works part-time, but used to work full-time, described what it can feel like to be a part-timer:

I think part-timers get left out of all sorts of things and you tend to get used as a general dogsbody because you only come in so many days a week. It's the same as they say, "Let the Saturday staff do it". You all like to be treated with respect as well. I do feel that you are left out of things.

Marjorie at the Superstore, who worked part-time as a shelf-filler, felt very badly about being, as she saw it, treated so much worse than the full-timers:

Well, we're (the part-timers) treated like

dirt. I mean the till girls they don't seem to
have all this trouble - I'm sure (the checkout
supervisor) doesn't talk to them as if they
were some old dog on the street.

Jo, too, felt that part-timers were looked down on:

They think because you got a couple of kids and
you're gonna work in the evening your brain's
gone, that's how they treat you, they think
you're a load of zombies. Very sarcastic in
the way they talk and things to you, it's
disgusting. They want you to do things for
them but they never show any appreciation for
it. Not even, "Thanks for that."

Of the women I interviewed, only two at the Superstore (Frances and Florence) and one at Roberts Bros
felt that there was no good reason why part-timers
shouldn't become supervisors at least. All the rest
shared the general consensus that somehow it
wouldn't work. The kind of beliefs I set out on
p.74 regarding part-timers and full-timers, seem
to be shared by management, as witnessed by the lack
of promotion opportunities for part-timers and the
women themselves. Given this and the fact that, as
I have tried to argue, the explanation for such
beliefs maybe has more to do with certain ideological structures than anything else, what are some of
the objective realities?
    There is a question of the formal rights and
obligations of part-timers. Anyone who earns less
than 32.50 pounds per week does not have to pay a
National Insurance contribution, and neither does
their employer. Also no one earning less than 34.41
pounds a week has to pay income tax (6). For the
employer, and - at least in the short term - the
employee therefore, it can be an advantage to keep
below these thresholds as, for example, is the case
with all the night-fillers at the Superstore.
    At the Superstore all employees who work more
than 20 hours per week are entitled to a certain
amount of sick pay after they have been employed by
the BCS for more than a year - the number of days
being increased with each year's service. Sick pay
is only paid when employees are absent because they
themselves are sick. Employees are allowed to take
leave of absence at the discretion of the management
if they have family problems such as a sick child,
but they will not be paid. Anyone, part-time or
full-time, who works a five-day week and who works a

Saturday is paid an unsocial working hours allowance. Entitlement to paid holidays is worked out on a ratio of days to the length of employment by BCS and the ratio is the same for part-timers as it is for full-timers. Anyone who works at Robert Bros as a part-timer has the same rights and entitlements as full-timers as far as sick pay and holiday pay are concerned; part-timers' entitlements being worked out on a pro rata basis depending on the number of hours they work.

It is perhaps worth making the very obvious point that the hours that nowadays constitute full-time would in the past have been part-time. Also, since both stores are open a good deal longer than thirty-nine hours per week, not even full-timers are there all the time. As regards the women I interviewed, at the Superstore half were full-timers and half part-timers, and at Robert Bros three of the women were part-timers. In terms of their attitude to their work there was no systematic difference between the full-timers and the part-timers; all the women who had, or expected to have families, put their commitment to their families before their commitment to their job, but given that, all were also conscientious at work and concerned to do a good job. Whether someone worked full or part-time seemed to be related to their family circumstances and the particular stage they had reached in the family cycle; those with pre-school children normally worked part-time while the full-timers tended to be unmarried, or, if married, childless or with older children. For both full-timers and part-timers it was crucial that their job could be fitted in with the needs of their family.

As regards trade union activity, it is interesting that the last union representative in the store - who left to look after an elderly relative and had not been replaced when I finished working at the Superstore - was a part-timer, and that while I was at the store, the most active union member among the Grade 4 and 5 workers was a woman who worked part-time. There was also Jo who, although she did not define herself as an active trade unionist, nevertheless, as I have already described, was the instigator of a successful group confrontation of management. But whereas there is little difference between the women who work part-time and those who work full-time, except for their family commitments, there is far more difference between men who work full-time and men who work part-time. The male part-timers at the Superstore fall exclusively into

two categories: young boys still at school or
college who work on Saturday, and elderly men who
have retired from a full-time job elsewhere. All
the male part-timers are classified as Grade 5. At
Robert Bros the only two male part-timers in the
haberdashery department are again youngsters still
at school.

Part-time work is an increasingly important
segment of the labour market. A recent report in
the Guardian is very revealing as to certain key
trends. According to recent figures there has been
at one and the same time both an increase in the
numbers of unemployed and in the employed. The
explanation for this strange phenomenon it seems is
that while large numbers of women, who were not
registered as unemployed, have found employment, a
number of full-time jobs have been lost, and this
number is close to the rise in the unemployment
figures. During the same period there has been an
increase of 1.3 million in the number of part-time
jobs; a figure which is close to the increase of
women entering the labour market (Guardian,
18.6.84). What seems to be happening in fact is
something of a radical restructuring of the labour
market with part-time work coming to occupy an increasingly central role.

The reason for the growth in part-time work has
more than a little to do with the underlying ideological notions about the nature of part-time work
which I have talked about in this section. The
history of the struggles over working conditions,
pay, protection of all kinds for employees, all
these have centred on full-time work. Part-timers
have benefited from the gains won by full-timers,
but in general it remains true that part-timers have
fewer rights in terms of such things as sick pay,
holidays, and have less legal protection at work. A
state of affairs which is lent support by the
general feeling that part-timers are not real breadwinners, but only working for a bit of pin-money,
and that they are not really committed to their job.
To employers, therefore, part-timers can represent a
docile, flexible and, in certain regards, cheaper
workforce, who can often be fitted in with the needs
of the labour process more easily than full-timers.
This is one dimension of the reality of part-time
work.

At present women are caught in something of a
vicious circle. According to the prevailing social
norms, which most women broadly accept, it is on
women that the primary responsibility for domestic

work in the home generally, and in particular child-care, falls. Paid employment for most women is something which is fitted round the needs of the family; it is the man of the family who is expected to be the main breadwinner. Apart from the small minority of women who can aspire to middle-class, professional 'male' jobs, the jobs that women can get are for the most part poorly paid with poor promotion prospects. Quite apart from any ideo-logical considerations of who should be the family breadwinner, generally it is a simple fact of life that a husband can command a higher salary than his wife, a fact that makes the traditional division of labour of husband: breadwinner, wife: homemaker and mother, seem no more than logical and sensible. As long as women are saddled with the main domestic responsibilities, however, their chances of gaining equality with men in terms of status and pay at work are slim. As far as people's thinking is concerned, both management and many women seem to be in agree-ment that while a man may by expected to have a career, only exceptional women, women who have clearly demonstrated that in the either/or choice of family or career, they have chosen the latter, can reasonably expect to be allowed the opportunity to have a career. And, practically speaking, a woman with family commitments faces all kind of diffi-culties to do with having to take time off when pregnant, and to look after small children, to be there when children are ill, the likelihood that she must uproot herself if her husband has to move because of his job, problems if she is expected to do overtime because she still has to fit her domes-tic chores in somewhere, and so on. Enveloping all these practical difficulties is a great fog of guilt that they may be failing their children and their families in some way, and this is something even the most successful and high status working mothers are seldom entirely free from, (see, for instance, Rapaport, 1976:308).
    Given the prevailing ideology the alternatives presented to women who have not renounced the idea of having children altogether, are on the one hand to be a wife and mother with a little part-time job which is fitted round the demands of the family, or on the other hand, to be a superwoman who combines career and family without sacrificing either; a woman who comes in from a hard day at the office and whips up a 'corden bleu' meal while changing the baby and helping little Johnnie with his homework.
    But perhaps things are changing. What my inter-

views seemed to indicate in terms of ideology is
that there is something of a disjuncture between
what people think is happening in society in general
- there it seems some sort of change is believed to
be taking place - and individuals' own beliefs and
ideas as these are manifested in their lives - where
unless a husband helping with the washing-up is
taken as signifying a radical restructuring of
domestic responsibility, not much in the way of
change seems to be occurring. However, one of the
important characteristics of any ideology, and this
factor should never be underestimated, is the way
even the most entrenched and apparently sacrosanct
beliefs can suddenly crumble if the objective social
structures reinforcing them change. The restructuring of the labour force I have mentioned is one of
the factors which may be eating away at the traditional sexual division of labour. What it is certainly doing is calling into question a lot of the
established ideas about the role of work in people's
lives and the kind of balance which ought to exist
between work and family life - this research project
is itself evidence of this questioning.

It is here that we come back to the significance of part-time work. For if one dimension of
part-time work is its potential as cheap, easily
exploited labour, at the same time it also has the
potential to open up a new way of approaching the
basic relationship between work and family life.
The fundamental shift which is needed to break the
vicious circle in which women are trapped, is to
break free from the established moral division of
labour between the sexes, so that it is no longer
the case that women must first and foremost be
mothers and homemakers, and, only after ensuring
that they adequately fulfil these roles are they
allowed to play a part in wage-earning social production. Similarly, men need to be freed from the
demand that first and foremost they should be breadwinners, and that only after this primary moral duty
has been fulfilled are they allowed to occupy themselves within the domestic sphere. Being a parent,
whether a mother or father, and being a productive
employed member of a society should not be either/or
choices, but should be seen as two aspects of life
which people should be able to combine without sacrificing either. One of the implications of this
is that the distinction between full-time and part-
time needs to be rethought, and there needs to be a
whole new range of more flexible working arrangements, free from the stigma currently attached to

work. Ultimately time management is not a question of how <u>individuals</u> budget their time between work and home, but how society sets up the relationship between the spheres of work and family.

SOME DETAILS OF THE WOMEN INTERVIEWED

Unless otherwise stated, all those listed as married are living with their husband and have their children living with them

## At the Superstore

| | |
|---|---|
| ANNE | 28 years old, married with two children aged three years and ten months, works 17 and a half hours per week as a shelf-filler. |
| APRIL | 22 years old, married, no children, works full-time in the butchery. |
| DENISE | 16 years old, unmarried, works full-time on the produce section. |
| DIANE | 32 years old, married with one child aged eight, works 17 and a half hours as a shelf-filler. |
| DOREEN | 29 years old, married (living with second husband), no children by this marriage (one child by first husband living with first husband) works full-time on the non-food section. |
| EILEEN | 33 years old, married with two children aged six and three years old, works 17 and a half hours per week as a shelf-filler. |
| ELSIE | 46 years old, married with two children, one of whom aged 16, lives at home, works 17 and a half hours as a shelf-filler. |
| FLORENCE | 45 years old, married with four children, all adult, one who lives at home, works 26 and a half hours as a till operator. |
| FRANCES | 23 years old, unmarried, works full-time on the delicatessen counter. |
| JANE | 31 years old, married with two children aged twelve and nine, works full-time on the delicatessen counter. |
| JO | 23 years old, married with two children aged eight and five, works 17 |

and a half hours per week as a shelf-filler.

KAREN  38 years old, divorced with one child aged 19, works 31 hours a week as a clerk in the office.

MARJORIE  40 years old, married (second husband, three children by first husband all of whom are with their father) with two children by this marriage who are five and four, works 17 and a half hours per week as a shelf-filler.

MAY  38 years old, married with two children, one who is grown-up and has left home and one aged 18, works 22 and a half hours in the butchery.

MONA  42 years old, married with one child aged ten, works 22 hours a week in the butchery.

PENNY  40 years old, married with one child aged 17, works full-time on the delicatessen counter.

PAT  31 years old, married with two children aged six and four, works 17 and a half hours per week as a shelf-filler.

ROSE  59 years old married with one child 18 years old, works 17 hours as a till operator.

SHARON  17 years old, unmarried, works full-time on the delicatessen counter.

TINA  16 years old, unmarried, works full-time and has been moved around several sections.

## At Roberts Bros

CAROLINE  25 years old, living with a partner, no children, works full-time.

DAWN  22 years old, unmarried, works full-time.

ELLA  55 years old, married with-grown up children living away from home, works full-time.

ELLEN  28 years old, living with a partner, works full-time.

FLORA  64 years old, widowed, two grown-up children living away from home, works 15 hours a week.

KAY  27 years old, married with one child

|        |                                                                                           |
|--------|-------------------------------------------------------------------------------------------|
|        | aged eight months, works 19 hours a week.                                                 |
| LAURA  | 56 years old, married with two grown-up children living away from home, works full-time.  |
| LESLEY | 18 years old, unmarried, works full-time.                                                 |
| MARIAN | 30 years old, divorced, no children, works full-time.                                     |
| SYLVIA | 55 years old, married with one grown-up child living away from home, works 20 hours a week. |

NOTES

1. I would like to thank the staff and management of the BCS and Roberts Bros for their enormous support and co-operation.

2. I also interviewed a small number of men, but I have not made use of these interviews in this report.

3. One shilling (1s) = five pence.

4. Since the completion of my fieldwork the BCS has decided to try the experiment of employing some trainee female butchers.

5. The training department makes a lot of use of video, filming the students who then have the films played back to them so they can see how they appear to others.

6. 1983 figures.

Table 2.1 - The Peacehaven Superstore Workforce

| | Women | | Men | | Total | | |
|---|---|---|---|---|---|---|---|
| | No. | % | No. | % | No. | % | % |
| Full-time (1) | 46 | 48 | 49 | 52 | 95 | 100 | 49 |
| Part-time (2) | 83 | 85 | 15 | 15 | 98 | 100 | 51 |
| Total | 129 | 67 | 64 | 33 | 193 | 100 | 100 |

(1) Full-time is a person working more than 30 hours per week. The standard full-time week is 39 hours.

(2) Part-time is anything less than 30 hours per week.

Chart 2.1: The Brighton & Hove Co-operative Peacehaven Superstore

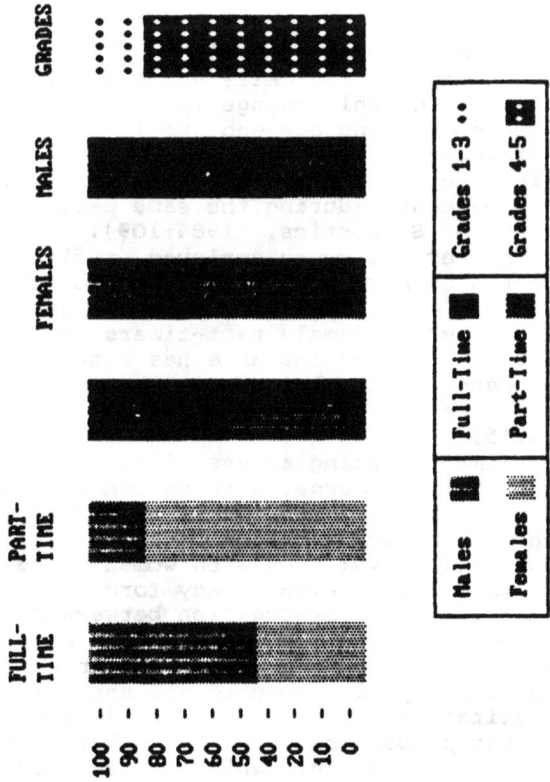

Chapter 3

MALE MANAGERS AND FEMALE EMPLOYEES

T.Scarlett Epstein

The climate of opinion within which women work has been changing radically since the last war. One indicator of this change is the growing number of women of working age who are in formal employment: it increased by 12 percent between 1972 and 1980 while the respective numbers for men decreased by two percent during the same period (Annual Abstract of Statistics, 1984:109). The increase in the number of women employed reflects a growing emphasis on part-time work. Most of the part-timers take up unskilled jobs in the service industries. The number of female part-timers engaged in retail distribution for instance has risen by as much as 7.5 percent in the one year between December 1982 and December 1983 (Department of Employment, 1984:15).

Women working as unskilled labour is not a new phenomenon of course. Working conditions altogether, and for women in particular, have fortunately become much more humane since the early days of the industrial revolution when women worked hard, even down the mines, without any formal or legal protection. Yet the segregation between male jobs and female jobs and the consequent concentration of females in a few occupations continues to keep women predominantly in low-paid and unskilled employment. 'In Britain about a quarter of all occupations have a higher proportion of women workers than the labour force as a whole, whilst three quarters of all occupations have a higher proportion of men workers than the labour force as a whole' (Martin, 1984:25). This means that men have a much wider choice of jobs while women are confined to a limited number of occupations.

This clustering of women within a few occupations is further exaggerated by vertical separa-

tion between men and women in the same occupation:
managers are almost always men who often supervise
female employees. The few women who have succeeded
in joining managerial ranks tend almost always to
supervise only women. Altogether female professionals are restricted for the most part to specialities
where most of their clients are women (paediatrics,
divorce litigation, domestic science teaching) or to
those completely removed from public contact (lab-
oratory and library work) (Caplow, 1954:230). Men
usually do not like to work for women. An extreme
view of this kind was some years ago (in 1971) put
bluntly by the personnel manager of a large British
firm when he said 'I'm an Englishman and I think
most people like me would never work for a woman or
a black' (Galenson, 1973:8). Though only few managers would these days still be prepared to make such
a discriminatory statement, the 'horizontal and
vertical separation between men and women at work
has changed very little over the last 80 years'
(Hakim, 1981). Women still constitute only a small
proportion of managerial staff.

Most employers these days claim that they are
keen to increase the proportion of women among their
managerial and supervisory staff, and many even
stress that they have gone out of their way to offer
managerial training specifically to help upgrade
their female staff. Yet this all seems so far to
have brought about only marginal changes.

Only a pitifully small number of women have as
yet joined managerial ranks. Of 10,000 recently
sampled British women none were working in general
management (Martin, 1984:23). There are of course
many reasons why women these days are still reluctant to try to become managers. In the previous
chapter Crehan shows that women, even if they do
have jobs, consider themselves first and foremost as
wives and mothers. 'The family comes first' is the
message that comes through loud and strong out of
all the interviews Crehan conducted with female
staff both at the BCS and at Roberts Bros. Of
course, this provides a useful excuse for employers
to continue excluding women from managerial staff.
What is often overlooked in this context is that
this argument only deals with the supply side of
female managers. But there are also strong forces
operating on the demand side to discourage women
from trying for managerial positions. While the
previous chapter focuses on British women working in
the retail trade and how they juggle their work and
home responsibilities, this chapter looks at the

other side of the coin. It explores the problem
from the vantage point of management. (1)

## IT'S EXPERIENCE THAT COUNTS

Each of the managers we interviewed maintained that
formal training is only marginally important to the
making of a good manager. John, (2) a Manager at a
large department store stressed:

> The best in depth managerial training is learn-
> ing by experience. It just does not happen at
> once, it takes time before a person acquires
> managerial skills. I am afraid that's got to
> be accepted. You can teach a system; put them
> in a class room and say "Here we are, this is
> the system, follow the pattern and this is what
> happens at the end of it"; it's fine if a
> person has got that sort of a mind, then fine
> they will learn it, but when it comes to the
> actual dealings with another human being, that
> can't be taught in the classroom; it's some-
> thing that has to develop and, indeed, has to
> be to some extent naturally within the
> individual's personality. I have been on many
> courses but I have never been on one that I
> could classify as being taught how to manage.
> I mean there are many courses, there are
> courses for assistant managers dealing with
> management and that sort of thing, and when you
> become department manager you get a few courses
> thrown in as well, but they are very few and I
> don't believe that any of them make you a
> better manager.

Most of the managers at the BCS have also learned
their jobs by experience. They are therefore
convinced that on-job training and hard work are the
ingredients which help to make a good manager. When
I asked Roy, a Senior Manager at the Peacehaven
Superstore, whether he intends to arrange for some
of his junior colleagues to go for managerial training he emphatically claimed that 'Our Junior
Managers could teach the trainers a lot. Altogether
I think the Co-operative Training College at
Loughborough would be well advised to come here and
see how things ought to be run. It would also be
better all round if the State would be run like our
Superstore, things would be a lot better then!'
Though John is not quite as critical of his firm's

management training, he too complains about the lack of sales skill and experience among the trainers:

> We don't have in our training department expert sales people, because they are not; they put things over, they are able to guide a particular programme or training session so that it develops and the natural process of learning takes place, but they are not sellers, you know.

John's perception of what is involved in managerial skills in retailing differs considerably from Roy's which, I would argue, reflects the different style of their respective firms' operations. For John a good manager is:

> A confident individual that has got the personality and the character, the enthusiasm, the willingness to tackle human relations in every sphere. Individuals with specialisation skills do not necessarily make potential managers, because they are best left as highly paid experts but they don't necessarily have a managerial skill.

John considers team leadership and all that this implies in terms of human relations, as the main role of the manager. By contrast, Roy puts much more emphasis on functional skills in judging managerial efficiency. For instance, he considers the ability to arrange attractive food displays a most important quality of a produce manager. The BCS food stores altogether pay only little attention to the importance of human contact in sales operations. It is argued that the large self-service arrangements in food stores eliminate the need for personal relations between sales staff and customers. By contrast, in many department stores, customers often seek advice from sales staff and make their purchases accordingly. John explained that:

> There are some customers who are demanding, there are people who can be absolutely exquisite and there can be people who are abominably rude and abusive, and unfortunately we are in the front line of all that. A sales manager has to be somebody who can handle these different types of customers and, more important, he should help his staff also to do so. I think it is the one thing that people will

judge you on: The skill of serving and dealing with customers, assisting them in a pleasant, efficient and satisfactory manner is indeed a skill and it's a skill which is obtained through experience.

Though John and Roy differ in their perception of managerial roles - John emphasises team leadership whereas Roy stresses functional performance - they both are convinced that it is experience that counts in management. This emphasis on learning by experience as an essential ingredient of a good manager seems at first sight to indicate equal opportunities all round. In fact it has an in-built bias against women. Most women have to interrupt their careers to start a family, therefore the process whereby they can learn by experience is automatically interrupted during the most important phase of their working lives.

The modal age of management staff at the Peacehaven Superstore falls between 18 and 23 years. Similarly, John said, 'The majority of people don't get promotion until they are 20. Twenty is probably a more realistic age for taking up promotion.' Therefore, it seems that round about 20 years is the age when individuals with management potential are differentiated from the rest of the work force. For young men of this age group new career prospects open up, disregarding whether or not they are married. By contrast, most girls between 18 and 23 are married and already have one or two small children, or they are planning to do so soon. We have seen in the previous chapter that not only does society expect women to subordinate their career aspirations to their family responsibilities, but they themselves give priority to having a family over having a satisfying job. Accordingly, labour force participation is highest among girls below 19 years; it falls for women between 20 and 29 years and rises again for women above 29 years (Martin, 1984:11). By contrast, male labour force participation continues to increase until 35 years of age, when it begins to decline slightly until 60 years, after which it drops radically (GHS, 1981:90). Since potential managers are spotted when they are about 20 years old, the chances for girls to be selected are rather remote. While the young male candidates for managerial positions can begin to acquire the necessary skills by on-job learning, women are pre-occupied with familial responsibilities.

Young women with managerial aspirations are forced to choose between a career and having a family. Helen, one of the few females in management positions at the Peacehaven Superstore, confirmed this:

> I have only recently been promoted. I am thrilled about my promotion, I don't want anything to interfere with my career now. Women have to choose between a career and motherhood. You cannot succeed both to be a good manager and a good mother. If I ever get married I won't want kids. Now that I'm a manager I want to put all my weight into my job. Maybe when I'm old I'll regret it, but I am still young now and I want to do what I want. I want to have a career rather than have a family.

This choice that women have to make between having a family or enjoying job satisfaction is reflected in fewer married women than single women being employed. As many as 82 percent of single women of all ages are employed, while only 60 percent of married/cohabitating women are economically active (Martin, 1984:12), and many of them work part-time only.

## PART-TIMERS CANNOT BECOME MANAGERS

Almost 60 percent of all women employed in retail distribution work part-time (DOE, 1984:S15). This high proportion of part-timers constitutes a further obstacle for women who have management aspirations. The managers I talked to at BCS and other retail firms were quite clear that having managers who worked part-time was simply not feasible. John replied to the question if he thought there was a chance for a part-timer to be promoted:

> Really in real terms, no. I don't really see that. Really part-timers, to me, they fit the need of the business because they actually fit into the business requirements, and secondly I believe it obviously suits them and I think there are no two ways about it. That's one way of looking at it. I know there might be other ways of looking at it, but you get no continuity. The trouble with this business is that you do need that. The person who is here for only three days, for example, I mean they could

93

do an actually admirable job on the days they are here but what happens on the days they are not here? What's the follow up? The business needs continuity and I'm afraid that's what a part-timer can't give you. I appreciate that you could have a noon to 4.00 p.m. part-timer and I suppose you could probably get away with it. You could probably get away with part-time assistant managers for example on the special sales team; that would probably work out because they would fit in on the day and there is no continuity required so there is an element for it here, but within my department I personally could not run my department with a part-time assistant manager. There must be, I'm sure, situations where you could. Being realistic, I myself couldn't do it.

Sheila, a part-time clerk at the Peacehaven Superstore, complains bitterly about the exclusion of women from managerial positions:

I don't see why most managers have to be men and most sales staff are women. Surely it should be possible for a woman to become a manageress. I have been working here as a clerk for five years; I am very keen to learn about other aspects of how this store operates, but I don't stand a chance because I'm only a part-timer. I work 28 hours per week. Five days every week I turn up at work at 8.45 in the morning and leave at two in the afternoon. On most days I am home when my children return from school. I think that every mother should look after her children rather than please herself and go out to work, at least until the kids are eight or ten years old. The store manager told me a few months ago that I could get a junior management position if I am prepared to work full-time. I have not yet been on any of the Co-op training courses because I am only a part-timer. I do think women should be given an equal chance - but of course as long as they have small kids they have to look after them. I don't think it's fair though that women have to choose between a career and their families. Men don't have to make this choice; men can have both a career and a family; for women it's either or. Perhaps things could be organised differently and women could have careers after their children are off their hands. Now that both my children are already a little older I am now thinking what should I do with the rest of my life. My husband is a lot older than I am, he will retire in two years, then I think I will want to work full-time. Maybe then I will get promoted. I wish I had more education, then things for me would not be what they are now. If I ever become a manageress I would treat all staff politely as human beings instead of bossing every one around, which is what most of the young managers here do. I really often do not know how some of the women who work on the shop floor put up with this kind of treatment.

Sheila's complaint expresses what so many other women like her feel. She obviously has managerial aspirations and, now that her children are already advanced in their schooling, she considers herself absolved of her overreaching family responsibilities. But having to work as a part-timer for so many years she has been out of the promotion stream. She never had a chance to learn management by experience, nor have her employers thought it worthwhile to send her for training just because she worked only part-time.

One way in which part-time managers could be introduced is through job sharing. But retail management in England still seems to be reluctant to experiment with job sharing. Many managers strongly oppose such a novel work pattern; one of them said:

No, I don't believe job sharing is possible. Not the way that we have to work here. Continuity does really mean that the individual has to follow it up. The handing over would really be very impersonal to the customer. I mean if the customer is dealing with somebody over a particular aspect, and that's the only area of continuity we have to worry about, then obviously one minute she is dealing with Joe Brown and the next minute she is with Ted Bloggs or whatever. Really that would seem very rude and unfair that you're sort of handing her from person to person. People would object to that. As far as the staffing is concerned, there is a great reliance and I don't care how well two people got on together, they are not totally going to agree; so one assistant manager is going to be saying one thing, one will be saying another and there will be conflict.

It is interesting to note here that this manager uses male names as example of job-sharing managers, while he refers to customers as females. This illustrates the deeply rooted assumption that managers in retail stores are mainly men while most customers are women. In his argument he rationalises his own aversion against part-time managers by claiming that such an arrangement would undermine the continuity essential in good sales management. He did not consider for a moment that no one full-time manager is on the job for the total store opening hours. Even full-time managers have in fact to pass on their problems to their colleagues. Altogether, the difference between part-time and full-time work can be very small in terms of hours but the divide between part-timers and full-timers is so great that it seems to overrule any objective consideration of how part-timers can best be absorbed into the overall employment pattern, particularly because most part-timers are women and most full-timers are men.

In view of the planned longer shop opening hours and almost certain Sunday trading, retailers will have to face this problem pretty soon. The trade unions are already worried what all this will involve for working conditions (see pp.189-190), but not even the unions are as yet prepared to take on board part-timers interests in the same way as they have become accustomed to represent full-timers. Part-timers working in retailing, most of whom are women, are therefore neglected and underprivileged. They are discriminated against by employers in terms of training and managerial promotion and they cannot count on full trade union support to fight their case (see p.184).


MANAGEMENT AND ITS MALE CULTURE

All the managers at the Peacehaven Superstore have worked themselves up from ordinary sales staff. Many of them have spent most of their working life with the Co-op. As Roy said:

    I have been with the Co-op all my working life
    and most of my family also worked at the Co-op,
    even my wife worked for the Co-op before we got
    married.  My father managed a Co-op store in a
    small town and I began to work part-time there

when I was 14 years old: I collected the coke,
lit the boilers, cleaned the windows, swept the
floors and did all sorts of jobs like that.
When I was only 19 years old I was offered the
job of managing one of the Co-op stores. This
was my chance and I grabbed it. Since then I
have moved to bigger and bigger stores until I
landed here at Peacehaven. It has meant jolly
hard work - when we first opened at Peacehaven
I used to leave home at about 6.30 in the
morning and did not get back till after mid-
night. There was so much to do, it was kill-
ing. The only break I took during the day was
to go with Harry, one of the other managers
here, for a drink at lunchtime. I'm sure that
these drinks helped keep our strength up.

Roy's style of life, his total commitment to his job
and his regular visits to the local pub, although in
tune with many male managers, differentiates him
from the way most women could or would want to live
their lives. Like so many of his managerial
colleagues he considers that work comes first, while
family responsibilities not only take second place
but also have to be subordinated to the demands of
the job. As we have already seen, most young women
are reluctant to allocate second place in their
lives to their family responsibilities. Women are
also not used to standing and drinking at bars as
men do (see p.200). What goes on around a bar is
exclusively male. Women are thus excluded from the
managerial network which relies heavily on men drinking together. Harry learnt a great deal from Roy
during their drinking sessions. No woman was so
privileged.

In his managerial role Roy insists that he
tries his best to promote women. This is in line
with overall Co-operative Society policy these days.
By contrast in his personal life he draws a clear
cut division between how men should behave and what
men should do:

I like my wife not working; I like her being at
home when I get back after work; it's nice to
have a meal waiting. Otherwise the kids would
also come home from school to an empty house.
It's nice to have a wife who looks after the
home. All I think about while I am at work is
this blasted place, but once I get home I
forget all about it.

Male Managers and Female Employers

This emphasis on different roles for men and women is reflected in his attitude towards promoting female staff to managerial positions. He is convinced that:

> Much fewer women than men have managerial potential. For instance, one of our young female staff seems ambitious, but she wants to be promoted before she has ever shown what she can do. I have been telling her that she must first show that she can increase sales, only then can she hope to get promotion, not before. Altogether I can usually smell it if anyone has managerial potential. Most working women give overrriding priority to their family commitments and if they don't they ought to! (He added with a smile)

At one level Roy accepts the need to have a majority of female staff working in Co-operative stores, at another level he considers it undesirable for women to take up formal employment at all, and certainly not jobs like management which he is sure would have an adverse effect on family life. He is convinced that job requirements are given and cannot be altered to harmonise better with family needs:

> I can get as many women working part-time mornings as I need, but not after two in the afternoon. If a woman wants to work only between 9.00 and 12.00 in the morning and the job requires her to work between 10.00 a.m. and 3.00 p.m., then I cannot employ her.

Roy obviously does not consider it possible to make any concessions to allow young women with small children to work in the Peacehaven Superstore. It is always the employee who has to adjust to work requirements; these requirements are seen as unalterably fixed and therefore cannot be adjusted to reduce the conflict with family commitments.

These managerial beliefs inevitably lead to many young men finding themselves in positions which give them control over older female staff. Depending on the personality of the individual concerned this induces these young managers either to be aggressive or to worry about having to order around women some of whom may be of their mother's age. Both these attitudes reflect a sense of insecurity on the part of young managers. Bill, one such junior manager who works at the Peacehaven

Male Managers and Female Employers

Superstore, confided:

> What worries me most in my job is that other
> people don't take me seriously; if I tell one
> or other of the women working in my section to
> do a certain job a certain way, they often
> laugh at me. I have heard them say that "He's
> still green behind the ears" or "Who's he to
> tell me what to do?"; sometimes even the whole-
> sale suppliers get at me for no reason at all.
> I guess this is because I am still so young.
> But that shouldn't make people criticise me
> without reasons.

In reply to my question how he can explain that most
managers in the store were men Bill said:

> I don't really know; I guess the higher-ups in
> the Co-op think that women don't make good
> managers. For instance, I know one woman who
> was keen to become manager of the section where
> I now work. She was very good in arranging the
> display and everything but she was not select-
> ed. I guess it was largely because she was a
> woman.

Bill continued explaining what he will do once he
will be older and in a more established managerial
position:

> First of all I would make sure to have more
> women in managerial jobs; they would make good
> managers I am sure. Better than any man.
> Secondly, I would appoint a manager to be re-
> sponsible for part-timers. This is what we
> miss most in this Store; the part-timers have a
> rough deal simply because there is no one
> manager responsible for part-timers.

At one level, Bill was thus greatly concerned about
what he considered as unfair treatment given to
female staff in general and part-timers in
particular. Yet when we talked about his own private life he related that his own mother had been at
home as long as he went to school. Only afterwards
did she go out to work:

> I never thought that anybody's mum went out to
> work; I guess that some of the mums of my
> school friends must have done. But I guess
> they worked part-time, so they were always home

> when we came home from school,

And he continued emphatically:

> And that is how it should be for everyone!
> Whenever I'll get married and my wife wants to
> go out to work I won't mind. Only when we have
> kids I'll insist that she stays home until they
> are old enough to look after themselves.

Bill, like so many of his male managerial
colleagues, thus has dual standards; while he wel-
comes and supports the idea of female managers, he
is still convinced that mothers of small children
must forego job satisfaction to look after their
homes. He does not seem to realise that the young
women he plans to promote to management position are
also likely to be mothers of small children and
their husbands, like Bill himself, may not agree to
their wives' continuing to work. These male managers, like Bill and Roy, thus preach one thing while
they practise another: they preach equal opportunities for women, but when it comes to their views on
women's roles they insist that women should forego
their careers to look after their families.

Tim, another young manager at the Peacehaven
Superstore, differs a lot from Bill in personality.
Youth and consequent lack of self-assurance makes
Bill more considerate and Tim more aggressive. Tim,
being proud that he pulled himself up by his own
bootstraps, criticises women in general for having
second-class brains:

> I am convinced that most of the women working
> at the Co-op come to work because they need the
> money; or maybe they want the money; some women
> come to work because they want to get out of
> their homes and want to meet other women. None
> of them is in the least interested in what they
> are doing at work. They don't care whether the
> firm makes a profit or not, whether it is run
> efficiently or badly. All that women workers
> are concerned with is themselves, nothing
> else!... Altogether women should not go out to
> work; they should stay home and look after
> their families. But I guess I realise that in
> the world we live in it is difficult to have
> all women stay home. I guess one has to accept
> the fact of life that even some young mothers
> of small children have to go out to work.

Tim, another of the young BCS managers, firmly believes in men and women having different roles to fulfil and that women on the whole are endowed with lower potential than men. This makes him contempt- uous of the female staff he has to supervise, which is greatly resented by many of the women who bitter- ly complain about his rudeness and authoritarian ways. Tim does not seem to consider at all that Co- op managers should try to encourage good labour relations. For him, as for many other male mana- gers, the main objective of his work is to help maximise shareholders' dividends. That in the pro- cess of this exercise workers and in particular females, have to participate he regards as an inevitable evil. How much better he would like it if his Store could be run with the use of robots only rather than human beings!

John, who also was convinced at one level that female staff in his firm have the same opportunities as men to reach top management positions, tried to explain why there are so few female managers:

> We've got a couple of executives buying who are female - the opportunities are there. Why there are so few women in top jobs? I can only believe that they haven't met the sort of needs and requirements that those jobs call for. Quite frankly, there are not that many positions once that pyramid gets to the very top. I suppose there are only about six people one can really consider in the top hierarchy of our firm. If we're thinking about the total executive of the company, that is to say its directors and its trading and so on, there is only a handful of those people, five or six to be precise. Because the individual carries some weight in trading, I suppose it always has been recognised as a man's world. It's interesting that the one female store director that I worked for did not have a family. All that has got to play a part in all this. The commitment to the firm at that level of manage- ment is very high and it has got to be faced that you are giving a great deal of your life when you get into that high a position in the firm. I think the female makes that decision, "No, I will not go that far, I have got this dual commitment." I think you can't get away from the fact that the female is susceptible to the family and leaving and everything else and that's when the career gets spoilt.

Thus it seems women are usually ruled out from top
management because of their family responsibilities.
Yet a considerable proportion of section heads, for
instance, are women, which can be explained in terms
of the differential skills men and women possess:

> I can never think of a male running lace and
> ribbons, it is a feminine inclined job and a
> female will have that delicacy, that softness
> and understanding for it, that no male with all
> the good will in the world could possibly lend
> himelf to. But I mean in clothes-care aids,
> for example, I would always see a male; well
> there are physical elements as well which have
> to be taken into consideration. If you look at
> some of the department managers you have some
> females running what I would call very mascu-
> line departments, but it depends how you inter-
> pret it. By masculine merchandise I mean any-
> thing that is more manly than feminine, in the
> sense that anything that is dainty is feminine.
> It would be very difficult to see a man on the
> fashion floor. But if you take electrical
> goods, for example, you naturally think because
> of all the bits and pieces, technology and all
> that, it should really be a male. But that's
> not so important these days. I think you could
> probably get away with it, a female could
> easily do the job because it really is an
> administration job and as long as they are
> capable of organising, well fine that's all.

It seems generally the case that:

> Women are preferred for work which is precise,
> delicate or especially monotonous...any job for
> which only women are employed is likely to be
> classified as delicate, or even as monotonous,
> because it is women's work...Even where crews
> are mixed in sex, as in the shoe industry, jobs
> continue to be separated. The possibility that
> the distinction is based upon attitudes rather
> than upon technical requirements is suggested
> by the fact that what is woman's work in one
> shoe factory may be man's work in another and
> vice versa (Caplow,1954:233).

Most male managers are obviously influenced by prevailing norms, which conflict with each other. They
thus veer between a professed egalitarian approach
to managerial potential possessed by both men and

women on the one hand, to on the other the customary
norms of identifying men with having physical
energy, technological understanding and leadership
abilities while women are weak, subordinated and
interested mainly in fashions. Management has for
so long been deeply embedded in a male culture that
it is likely to take a long time before this will
change and individuals will be encouraged to
realise their potential and fulfil their aspirations
rather than be slotted into jobs and roles according
to their sex.

FEMALE MANAGERS IN A MALE CULTURE

For reasons already discussed, the few women who
succeed in getting promoted to managerial jobs are
either unmarried, without any family commitments, or
they are older women whose children are already
grown up and who therefore feel free to shed much of
their family responsibilities. Elizabeth, who had
only recently been promoted to a managerial position
at the BCS store, falls into the latter category.
She is now in her late forties. She got married
when she was 19 years old and had her children while
she was still very young. 'It's good to be a young
mother, you can grow up with your kids.' She was
emphatic about mothers of small children not going
out to work:

> Small kids should never be left alone - play
> school is okay for a few hours a week but every
> kid needs its mother. I began to work part-
> time when my youngest was five years old, but I
> worked such hours that I was always home when
> my kids got back from school.

Now her children are of course already grown up and
she even has grandchildren. Even though her children were no longer small when she began working
full-time at the Peacehaven Superstore, her husband
was not pleased about her having to work Saturdays:

> But he did not try to stop me. I can tell you
> no woman can keep a job down unless she has a
> supportive husband. If you don't agree at home
> you can't be good at work. I am lucky I have a
> supportive husband. He helps a lot in the
> home. Fortunately we like fish and chips so we
> often buy our evening meal. We don't have to
> bother about buying in food a lot and cooking

> meals. We just go out and buy it all at our
> local fish and chip shop.

Elizabeth counts her blessings for having a supportive husband. But she does not seem to realise that
she too in her supervisory capacity has absorbed
many of the male managerial values and attitudes.
Having said that women with small children should
work only part-time, if they take up jobs at all, in
her role as supervisor she complains about the lack
of job commitment among part-time women workers.
She presently supervises 43 female staff, half of
whom are part-timers, and she bitterly complains
that:

> Part-timers usually insist on finishing dead on
> time; while full-timers are prepared to stay a
> little longer if necessary. For instance,
> after the store has closed, but while there are
> still customers about, it is important for my
> staff to be around until the last customer has
> left. But I can get only full-timers to hang
> on a little after the end of their working day.
> Part-timers don't seem to care. They just dash
> off as soon as the bell has gone.

Therefore she too, like her male managerial
colleagues, applies different standards to women in
their roles as mothers on the one hand and in their
roles as workers on the other. While she is
convinced of the importance of children never to be
left alone, she criticises the young women she
supervises for insisting to leave work dead on time.
Many of these women do so solely to keep to their
child-caring arrangements. Otherwise their carefully organised childcare may be threatened and
their children would suffer. Elizabeth has thus
fully absorbed the male work ethic and preaches one
thing while as manageress she practises another.
Galenson neatly sums up the dilemma women face if
they aspire to managerial jobs:

> For a woman to become a manager, she must be
> able to show that she is capable of achieving
> something, but she must not be too involved in
> her career. If she were, she would not be a
> real woman. She must be more capable and more
> knowledgable than the average of her male
> rival. But she must not show it. She must of
> course have a husband. If she doesn't then she
> may be suspected of going in for management

because she cannot catch a man.  She must have
children, preferably several.  If she has no
children she may be suspected of devoting herself to management because she cannot devote
herself to children.  But if she does have
children why has she entered management?  Why
doesn't she look after her children?  She must
be a bad mother.  So how can she be a good
manager? (1973:8)

Management is still generally perceived as a male
world.  If women want to become managers they are
expected to behave like men; they have to play the
'managerial game' according to the established
'male' rules.

NOTES

1. The discussion presented here is based on
free-ranging interviews conducted with managers at
the BCS and other retail firms.  I am greatly
indebted to all those informants who were prepared
to share with me their experiences and thoughts in
the context of work and home life. With the approval
and encouragement from the executives of the firms
we studied, interviews took place within working
hours in rooms specially made available for the
purpose. I am extremely grateful for this generous
support and willing co-operation.
2. Pseudonyms have been used to hide the real
identity of our informants.

PART THREE

WOMEN IN THE RETAIL TRADE
(WEST GERMANY)

Chapter 4

THE GERMAN DEBATE

Jurgen Sass

BALANCING FAMILY AND WORK LIFE -
AN ISSUE PARTICULARLY RELEVANT TO WOMEN

In all industrialised countries women's increasing
participation in the labour force, especially on the
part of women with children, has given the problem
of compatibility of family and work life a new
urgency. For the last eighty years the rate of
female employment in West Germany has shown a surprising stability. During this period almost half
the women of working age have had some form of paid
employment (1).
    Within this relative stability, however, there
have been some considerable changes. As a result of
a higher school-leaving age and longer vocational
training women, especially since the early 1960s,
are entering the labour force later, while older
women are leaving earlier because of the lowering of
the age of retirement; at the same time the proportion of married women who are employed has risen
sharply, especially in the last 35 years. Whereas in
1950 married women made up 26 percent of the workforce, by 1982 the percentage was almost 48 percent.
Particularly significant is the increase in the
proportion of working women with children under 16
years of age in the last 20 years, which has risen
from 34 percent in 1961 to 43 percent in 1982
(BMJFG, Frauen in der Bundesrepublik, 1984:32).
Approximately 60 percent of women in employment in
West Germany today are married.
    These figures show clearly that the issue of
how to combine family and work life has become
increasingly important for women in recent decades.
The sharp increase in the number of women in part-
time employment (from 6 percent in 1960 to 30 percent in 1982) is evidence of one effect this problem

has on the labour market. There have been various attempts to alleviate the problem such as by increasing the number of childcare facilities and the introduction of maternity leave (1979).

This is not merely some debate among academics. During the last ten years or so the issue of women, employment and family has become an increasingly important question within the political parties, parliament, the feminist movement, and indeed among the public at large (see Family Report of the Federal Government, published since 1972). Of growing importance within this debate has been a concern at the rise of unemployment among women, which is higher than that for men; and at both the increase in part-time employment and at the relatively poorer working conditions and curtailment of rights associated with part-time work. In addition there is the proliferation of systems of flexible working of different kinds, which usually affect women first. On the ideological level, these developments are accompanied by a debate about what is the 'right' integration of women into the sphere of formal employment and social production.

Conservative politicians call for a strengthening of the family. They point to the rising divorce rate, the numerous problems among young people such as drugs, and also to the continuing decline in the birth rate. They also argue that stronger support for the family will ease the strain on public spending by reducing the need for expensive social services, the rising cost of which, it is claimed, can no longer be met by the state. The social services they are thinking of here are those concerned with childcare, care of the sick and ageing, the responsibility for which has always, to a large extent, rested with the family.

In practical policy terms what this means is demands (and actual legislation) for parental leave even for those parents - both fathers and mothers - who are not in paid employment, increased financial support for families with several children, government loans for married couples, encouragement of part-time employment and so forth.

On the other side of the political spectrum, the trade unions, the Social Democratic Party, and a large part of the feminist movement fear that such policies would only worsen the already existing inequality between men and women. They argue that such measures would force women out of the labour force, thus reinforcing the existing sexual division of labour between the unpaid labour of the domestic

sphere and paid employment in the world of social production. They call for increased integration of women into the labour force, a reduction of part-time employment and systems of flexible working, and a reduction of the normal full-time working week from 40 to 35 hours.
An empirical study focusing on these issues was carried out at the Beck department store in Munich. Since it is only concerned with a single case study, in no way is it suggested that its results can be taken as a respresentative statistical sample. Nevertheless, however, the study does provide a compelling and concrete example of the basic problems women face in trying to combine family and work life.


TIME AND WOMEN'S LIVES

When we talk today of the loosening of the formerly rigid work patterns, whether we are talking about the daily, weekly or yearly work schedules, or even the pattern of the working life as a whole, it is often forgotten that systems of flexible working are already very much with us. There is part-time work, working at home, shift work, and flexitime systems. Apart from shift work, which 6 percent of employed women work compared with 10 percent of men, women are the ones most affected by systems of flexible working (BMA, 1981). Systems of flexible working are essentially nothing new for women; they have always sought flexible arrangements to help them combine family and work life. Indeed, this dual role may depend on some form of flexible employment. The daily routine of a working woman who also has a family and children to care for is determined to no small extent by the dimension of time. If she is to accomplish everything, she must budget her time exactly; but she must also be flexible, since she is, so to speak, expected to be available around the clock. The rapid growth of part-time employment in the past 20 years shows clearly what a great need there is on the part of women for more free time and flexibility. The flexible organisation of time plays an important part throughout a grown woman's entire life, not only at work or with her family. While continuous full-time employment is the main characteristic of men's working lives, it is discontinuity and the simultaneous paid and unpaid work of job and family which is typical for most women, although in very different combinations.

It may be a simultaneous combination of both (e.g. part-time work), or it may be moving between periods of full-time employment and periods of time spent without a job, but working (unpaid) caring for a family. To sum up, flexible budgeting of time, both on a day-to-day basis and throughout life, seems a matter of course for women, and has been for long before the topic became such a focus of political debate. Calls for changes to lessen the disadvantages and strains of this way of living and the working conditions connected with it have seldom been voiced by women; and when they have, it has only been from a defensive position. An example of this is the stand taken by the trade unions regarding part-time work. For years they have justifiably criticised the poor conditions and the other problems associated with this type of employment, but only now have they begun to think about ways of including part-time work in wage agreements.

The question as to the pattern of work hours that people will, or should, work in the future always also involves some kind of qualitative evaluation of what happens during these hours, taking into account here both directly and indirectly productive work. Such assessments necessarily involve a considerable subjective element, depending as they do on what particular values are seen as most important. Which values come to be dominant in a society cannot be separated from questions of power.

For material and other reasons most women either have to, or choose to, inhabit both the world of home and family, and that of paid employment, but these two spheres have very different sets of values; morally and socially they may enjoy equal recognition, but not financially or economically. It is paid employment with its specific logic that is the main reference point for the dominant values in society. The logic and values of other social institutions, such as the family, are subordinated or ignored.

For most women the family is both a place where they perform important, if unpaid, work and the source of a kind of emotional experience that cannot be found in employment. This is evidently not the case with men. Who has ever heard men complain of the double burden of job and family, of the problems in readjusting to a job after a time at home, or about the recognition, or non-recognition of their work in the household? The problem of combining paid work with a family is mainly a problem for women, not men.

The German Debate

The fact that women are equally concerned and
identified with both the domestic and public domain
often rebounds on them by causing the problems they
experience to be seen as special 'women's problems'
which are often discussed and argued about without
there being any consultation with women themselves.

THE NEGATIVE VALUE GIVEN TO WOMEN'S WORK

No matter what sort of life a woman lives, and
whether she has freely chosen it or she has no other
option, or more likely some mixture of the two, she
can be sure she will be criticised. A mother who
works full-time is considered a bad mother, a woman
doing part-time work to be undermining full-time
jobs, and a woman who doesn't work outside the home
is said to be reinforcing the disadvantaged position
of women in society. This manifests itself subjectively in many women in a sense of guilt, reluctance
to push their own demands, and a general insecurity
about living according to their own sense of themselves.

If these judgments were only meant as a criti-
cism of the living and working conditions of women
at home or at work, there would be no problem. On
the contrary, help and solutions are just what women
need. The problem, however, is that the prevailing
attitudes to women's work leads to women valuing the
ideals and interests of others as the only right
ones and subordinating their own. The life of women
who stay at home, for example, is often said to be
a state predominantly characterised by isolation,
financial dependence on the husband, and lack of
social recognition, with no possibility of self-
fulfilment. The only solution offered by proponents
of this thesis is continuous full-time employment.
But what is the actual situation of these fortunate
ones? Most women work in unskilled jobs, have little
job security, receive lower pay, have little chance
of promotion, and suffer from isolation. In addition, the specifically female characteristics attri-
buted to them (resistance to monotony, dexterity,
flexibility and so on) are exploited by employers.

What should women in this situation do, choose
the frying pan or the fire? Must they wait for the
much-publicised long-hoped-for emancipation finally
to arrive?

It would be unjust not to recognise the efforts
of the trade unions to improve women's working conditions, but it may be difficult to convince women

that only by full-time employment is it possible to achieve self-fulfilment and self-realisation, if at the same time conditions at work result in just the opposite, and given the fact that none of this is likely to change in the foreseeable future. All things considered, it might be even more difficult to demand solidarity from women in ensuring job security for all full-time workers since this tends to mean in practice for all men. Solidarity here would mean foregoing all types of part-time flexible and variable working patterns.

Here, however, trade unions are ignoring both reality and the interests of most women. Women do not measure a full-time job by promises that may be redeemed sometime in the distant future, but rather on the actual daily work routine. And then household chores, part-time work, and flexible working hours represent thoroughly acceptable alternatives if the demands of combining job and family are to be met.

If the trade unions, with their claim to be the sole representatives of workers, really want to represent the interests of <u>all</u> workers, then they cannot reject outright every type of flexible working hours and part-time work. By doing so they ignore the vital needs of several million women who either already do not work a standard full-time week or who would like this option. Present trade union policy practically forces women to work full-time or not at all, because all types of interim solutions, such as flexible working hours, are seen as undermining the unions' goal of a reduction of the full-time working week.


THE DOMINATION OF MALE VALUES

The private household and women's work in the home have been the subject of much public disagreement in recent years. The new-found interest in this topic is probably due on the one hand to the policy now being pursued by conservatives which, because of the present recession, aims to shift social services back to the private sector so as to ease the burden on public expenditure and in some way compensate for cutbacks in various social services. On the other hand, it is the feminist movement which has been especially important in focusing debate on the sphere of domestic labour. It is generally accepted that the efforts to secure equality for women in the public sphere, at work, and in education can only proceed gradually, and that the double

burden of job and family will continue to be a reality for most women. Therefore, a policy for women
must include both domains. Increasingly feminists
are pointing out that home and family can, and do,
mean more to a person than just a place to renew
his/her working capacity. Complementary to the world
of employment, and viewing this domain with a critical eye, is the domestic sphere where it is personal
relationships and the emotional dimension of life
that are central. Because the domestic sphere demands so much of women, women themselves are probably quite well aware of the importance and value of
their 'work' within the realm of feelings and emo-
tions however little such work has been valued in
the public domain of formal employment.

Up to now this particularly female area of work
has been practically ignored in the debate surround-
ing domestic labour within the family and its relationships to formal employment; it does not fit into
the accepted distinction between blue-collar and
white-collar work within which debates about employment tend to be framed. The failure to recognise the
importance of this specifically female area of expertise is reflected in the excessive stress trade
unions, and even many feminists, put on full-time
paid employment. Paid employment, as it currently
exists, is organised predominantly on the basis of
male values and male logic, so that the demand that
all women should have full-time paid employment
amounts to saying that women should become like men,
but without ever quite achieving the position of
men. It would mean women giving up part of their own
female identity without receiving any adequate
recompense at the workplace.


THE FUTURE

The purpose of this study is to highlight certain
gaps in the debate about future forms of employment.
We have deliberately chosen not to look at the
question of the nature of the labour market. In
order to avoid any misunderstandings it should be
stressed that we are not saying that paid employment
for women is not important; undoubtedly, if women
did not participate in the labour force, their
chances of emancipation would certainly be even
smaller and much of what has already been achieved
by women would not have been. The reality lived by
most women calls for solutions that enable women to
live as they themselves want and need to live.

The German Debate

Such solutions should include flexibility as regards to time spent at work and in the domestic sphere. The questions to ask are: who will benefit from such flexibility, how will it be used, and what will it add to the quality of life? The replies of the women questioned in our study are perfectly clear: they want more time for their relationships and for their family. They want more consideration for their family problems at their workplace so that, for instance, it is possible to discuss family matters there without feeling guilty about it, but they also want to be able to live according to their own values in their job. The great satisfaction expressed as regards the flexible work-time scheme and the family-orientated atmosphere of the store studied, especially by part-time employees, shows that things can be done differently.

There are of course still many unsolved problems at Beck, for example among single parents who have to work full-time and who badly need more time off. Another unsolved problem is the question of promotion for women. Under present conditions, promotion involves sacrificing private life and family life. When solutions are proposed to help women who want promotion, or who are already in executive positions, it would be wrong simply to copy male promotion patterns. New strategies geared to the needs and wishes of women are needed. A start has already been made. There is, for example, job-sharing or paid periods of leave which can be used for a period spent at home with the family. In addition to this, a recognition and revaluation of the specifically female qualifications in the world of paid employment is needed. Why shouldn't the ability of shop assistants, for instance, to communicate be recognised and paid for in the same way as are the qualifications of a construction worker? These and other possibilities should be developed further, but always bearing in mind the chances and risks they involve for women.

What seems important to us if the conflict of interest, both now and in the future, between the family and the working world is to be solved, is that different approaches are adopted for the many different kind of problems that exist. It is crucial that the very diverse interest of different women be taken into account when suggestions are made or new practices instituted. One need only think of wives with children, single mothers, and young women seeking training to realise how diverse these interests are. Part of this approach involves ceasing to des-

116

cribe the work done by women within the family and
household as non-work; a formulation which is merely
another, further discrimination against women in
addition to those of the world of employment. As
long as it continues to be unrecognised and un-
respected that women's identities can be derived
from both family and job, and that women frequently
want both family and job, women will be the losers
in the game for social power and political in-
fluence, a game whose rules are largely written by
men.

## NOTES

1. Proportion of Women of Employable Age
Working in Gainful Activity (1907 - 1939 German
Reich; 1950 - 1982 Federal Republic of Germany)

| Year | 1907 | 1925 | 1939 | 1950 | 1960 | 1970 | 1982 |
|------|------|------|------|------|------|------|------|
| Percentage | 45.0 | 48.2 | 49.7 | 44.4 | 48.0 | 46.2 | 51.0 |

Source: A.Peters, Frauenerwerbstatigkeit. Literatur-
dokumentation des Instituts fur Arbeitsmarkt und
Berufsforschung, Nurnberg (LitDokAB S4/1984), p.3

Chapter 5

THE BECK DEPARTMENT STORE: A CASE STUDY (1)

Annemarie Gerzer

THE 'BECK MODEL': A PORTRAIT OF THE COMPANY

The company 'Ludwig Beck am Rathaus Eck' is a family
company which has been based in Munich since 1861.
The company developed from a haberdashers business
which was commissioned by King Ludwig II of Bavaria
to provide the furnishings for his castles. The
company is now a modern fashion department store
with its own distinctive character. After the Second
World War, the head of the company, Gustav
Feldmeier, rebuilt the store in the centre of
Munich. His management style was paternalistic and
he continued the traditional association of the
company with Bavarian art and culture, an association that was reflected in the goods sold by the
store. The late Mr Feldmeier is still well remembered as a patron of the arts in the Munich area.
   There was an important change in the fashion
industry in the late sixties once the post-war demand had been met: meeting basic <u>needs</u> was no longer
enough, now it was also important that stores were
able to satisfy consumer <u>demands</u>. As a result, Beck
completely rethought its range of goods and there
was a new emphasis on how the goods were displayed.
A study was conducted which found that although Beck
had a loyal, upper middle-class clientele, it had
very few of the modern goods demanded by the post-
war generation, in particular by the 'newcomers'.
This marked the start of a general restructuring of
the company both in terms of ownership and management - it is now owned by 12 partners - and also as
regards the company style and range of goods (see
Chart 5.1). A happy medium was found between retain-
ing its establishment image and yet managing to
introduce a cosmopolitan, trendsetting flair. The
Managing Director formulated the new company philo-

118

sophy as follows: 'The company must be more than a shop. It must express an attitude to life.' The most important principle of this new philosophy is: 'The customer is a guest; we want to play the role of host and not only sell, but also create an enjoyable and tempting atmosphere.' This philosophy has taken the place of the slogan more usual in the retail trade: 'The customer is always right.' The idea was that employees should think of themselves as mirror images of the clientele the company was aiming at and that they should identify with the company image. Beck sales staff should be able to give customers the information they need, advice on the latest fashions, but, above all, they should relate to the customers as people. This company philosophy is also based on the belief that a person should be able to develop herself to the full within the framework of her job and that she should be allowed to have a say in what affects her at the workplace.

In 1976 a survey of female employees found that 39 percent of full-timers wanted to work less than the 173 hours, which was the monthly average they were then required to work, and that even among those who were already working part-time, 21 percent would have liked to reduce their hours even further. The survey also found that many of the employees wanted a more flexible work schedule. This shows clearly how women, particularly in their classic conflict of trying to combine job and family obligations, consider it very important to have flexible working hours. Another aim of the new company policy was to match staffing levels with customer demand. Customer frequency had been measured so that there was reasonably precise information with which to plan optimum deployment of personnel. The measurements showed that at that time too many people were being employed at times such as the early morning, when there were not many customers, while at other times, for instance lunchtime, there were fewer employees but many more customers. A new individual worktime (IWT) scheme was devised on the basis of these findings in collaboration with the works council and employees.

THE IWT SCHEME

Every employee is able to decide in advance how many hours per month she wants her average worktime to be. The lower limit is 60 hours and the upper, which constitutes full-time, is 173 hours per month.

The Beck Department Store: A Case Study

Between these two limits any number of hours can be selected in steps of ten hours, with anything less than 173 hours being classified as part-time. The department in which the employee works must be consulted as to how the agreed number of hours is to be distributed over the month. The particular needs of the department, or the employee, may mean that in certain months an employee works less than her agreed average, but this does not affect her monthly salary. These hours can be made up during the next few months, for example during the Christmas period. Overtime worked, so-called 'time credit', can also be used to advantage in less busy periods by taking free time.

Planning charts in each department show how many staff hours are required to ensure that, given a specific turnover and normal conditions, customers receive a proper level of service. These figures can be very different for different departments, and at different times of the year. The department uses the customer frequency table to determine how best to distribute staff hours over the day. In addition, a minimum staffing level is agreed on with each department for the early morning hours. Together with the department management, the company management compiles an approximate turnover plan for each month. Long-term plans are always elaborated a week in advance. This plan lays down the free time schedule and also stipulates which saleswomen are to be absent during which periods. Time worked is recorded by a central computer via electronic time-keeping equipment. Each employee is able to check how many hours she has actually worked and the hours she has in deficit or credit at these time-keeping points. This electronic time-keeping system not only permits the company to keep track of when employees clock in and out, it also enables them to determine exactly what the ratio of sales staff is on a day to day basis. Providing the minimum staffing levels laid down by the company are met, breaks - so employees can do their shopping, have a smoke or whatever - can be taken as frequently as required during working hours, after consultation with the department. These breaks are then recorded as free time.

The IWT scheme does not affect the collectively bargained agreements currently in force and all legal and collectively bargained regulations regarding maximum working times, breaks, legislation on children and young persons and maternity leave continue to apply. The part-timers receive the same social benefits as full-timers on a pro rata basis

and are integrated in the training and further-training system. Initially, approximately 60 percent of the workforce took up this new work time offer and now the IWT scheme has become standard for all employees.
The attractiveness of the IWT scheme and the family-orientated atmosphere at Beck are certainly two of the reasons why employee turnover at Beck is very low.

## ATTEMPTS BY BECK TO IMPROVE THE STATUS OF SALESWOMEN

### Cultivation of the Saleswomen's Image and Status at Beck: The Creation of a Professional and a Female Identity

Our study established that one of the most important sources for the self-definition of saleswoman at Beck was the special status accorded to the saleswoman within Beck; in general the job of saleswoman, like so many jobs associated with women, does not enjoy a very high social standing. It is not only men who consider the professional status of saleswoman to be low; many women also dismiss the job of saleswoman as being a dead end as far as any kind of female emancipation is concerned. What is demanded of a saleswoman tends to be seen as essentially no different to what is demanded of any woman so that, as Horath puts it:

> The similarity of their job to their life outside work can make it difficult for young women to think of their job as any kind of profession and to see their training as meaningful. If professional life only requires what any woman can do anyway, what is the point of training? (Horath and Muller, 1984:20).

The qualities expected of a saleswoman could also be seen as a list of complementary or alternative qualities to those associated with what is thought of as the typically male professional qualities such as competitiveness, toughness and self-assertiveness:

> In order to work as a saleswoman, a woman must have a good command of language, memory for people and numbers, must be attentive, be able to adapt and establish a rapport easily, be self-confident, polite, patient and self-com-

121

posed. (Professional image of the salesman/ saleswoman).

However, the so-called 'female qualities' still count for little in the world of employment so that women are faced with various choices if they want to participate in this world:

1. To adapt entirely to the male ethos and, consequently, partially disown their female identity.
2. To reassess the work they are paid to do on the basis of their own system of values and to bring to their job to invest the wealth of experience they have gathered from family life.
3. To exclude themselves from the 'professional' sphere.

If these really are the only three options, then we have returned to the cleavage of the 'working woman' versus the 'housewife', with the 'working housewife' somewhere in between.

In respect, Beck seem to have found a better balance than many companies. It not only employs 'working housewives' but, very importantly, also women who consciously think of themselves as identifying equally with their family and their job.


'THE CUSTOMER IS OUR GUEST' NOT 'THE CUSTOMER IS ALWAYS RIGHT'

By replacing the slogan 'the customer is always right' with that of 'the customer is our guest', Beck has helped its saleswomen to think of themselves in a new and more positive way. They see themselves, and are expected to see themselves, as the customers' equals, not as subordinates. This was reflected in the fact that whereas those questioned considered the image of saleswomen in general to be somewhat negative, they felt the image of Beck sales staff was a much more positive one.

Enjoying meeting people was one of the qualities saleswomen at Beck considered most necessary for their job, and it was also one of the aspects of their job that they felt came most easily to them; the Beck philosophy, it was felt, enabled them to use their social skills in a different and less demeaning way. One employee who has been with the company for five years put it like this:

The Beck Department Store: A Case Study

> When I worked in another store, I was not able
> to protect myself against the often excessive
> demands of the customer. I always had to be
> friendly and helpful even if it meant that I
> felt I was selling myself. Nowadays it is quite
> different. I feel as if I don't have to put up
> with being deliberately annoyed and I can stand
> up for myself. I am confident that my bosses
> will support me if I open my mouth when custo-
> mers are being stupid. Now I am also not afraid
> of sometimes telling customers the truth and I
> don't just have to grin and bear it. I feel
> that I have a great deal more freedom now and I
> don't feel as if I need to hide my feelings
> just because of the company. It also affects
> the way I approach customers since I now feel
> so self-confident.

This self-confidence is a matter of course to the
young saleswomen who have now trained at Beck:

> I am going to stay with this job. I like it a
> lot and I don't take any stick. The older
> saleswomen thought something else: to play a
> subservient role and serve above all else. Of
> course I also realise that the overall image of
> women has changed, yet that's what I like so
> much about Beck: they give me a strong, posi-
> tive female image.

Being a Specialist

Another important component of the positive image
Beck saleswomen have of their job is their specialist knowledge and the way they use this to advise
customers. After 'enjoying meeting people', specialist knowledge was considered to be the second most
important quality that sales staff need (see Table
5.3). In contrast to the self-service trend of the
seventies, Beck still attaches great importance to
advising customers and this means that sales staff
need to be properly qualified. 86 percent of the
female employees questioned had finished an apprenticeship either in the retail trade or in a profession related to the retail trade. Their professional training, and the possibility of using it
at work, is what gives them their self-confidence.
One statement is representative of many in this
respect: 'It is not just serving someone, it is the
specialist knowledge which counts.' The saleswomen
see their role as being to advise and help the

The Beck Department Store: A Case Study

customer rather than simply selling at all costs,
and this relieves a certain amount of pressure, even
if the financial incentive still remains since the
saleswoman receives a bonus on sales, and given the
low basic wage it is necessary that they <u>do</u> sell. As
one saleswoman commented:

> To me, it is important that we do not <u>have</u> to
> sell something. I have a far better relation-
> ship with the customer and am able to enjoy
> this without feeling bad if I have sold no-
> thing. This gives me greater freedom and
> customers are also more honest and friendly.

Selling is more than just marketing goods. It also
involves a lot of public relation work, particularly
in the case of some employees:

> I see one of my strengths as being my ability
> to handle difficult customers and I get an
> enormous amount of satisfaction from dealing
> with them on a one-to-one basis. This human
> dimension is far more important to me than
> selling itself and I like the fact that I can
> do this at Beck. I try and advise people in a
> broad sense: being able to relate to the indi-
> vidual, finding out exactly what she wants,
> which often involves not only relating mentally
> but also emotionally, but I always find it
> personally satisfying. Selling is perhaps the
> result of establishing this kind of relation-
> ship.

This shows the value there can be in allowing the
individual a certain freedom and runs counter to
assumptions about the 'stereotyped role behaviour of
a saleswoman's personality' (Mills, 1955). Because
she is able to use her entire personality in her
job, the Beck saleswoman has a positive self-image.
The value the company gives to training and specialist qualifications is also reflected in the image
the Beck saleswomen have of their job.

EMPLOYEES REFLECT CUSTOMERS

Beck believes that the necessary degree of honesty
in selling can only be produced by personally upgrading the saleswoman as a woman, person and qualified specialist. One way the company attempts to
achieve this upgrading is by participating in the

124

discussion groups that have been set up by various management organisations within the retail trade which are intended to promote a new image for saleswomen, analogous to the new image of the trained female bank clerk. Employees from a number of different companies take part in these discussions. The Managing Director sees it as very important to work at making the saleswoman more self-confident in order to counteract the typical woman's image - to be subservient and keep quiet:

> I find this image a great shame and it is time that it was done away with. We want to support our people here and put into practice the motto 'the customer is a guest', stressing that the host is on par with her guest.

The company offers comprehensive training to this end, aimed at the entire personality, not only at improving sales performance. Honesty is important if the host is to be genuine. If there is a conflict between the saleswoman and the customer, the saleswoman should still feel secure enough to stand her ground: at that particular moment, 'I am a person' is more important than subordination to the customer, even though this might be more conducive to sales. All this, however, should also involve an openness and willingness to learn in an atmosphere of tolerance and self-confidence since 'helping the customer' is such an important part of the sales assistant's job. This is the aim of the Beck training. Since there is such a strong emphasis on the personal relationship between staff and customers at Beck, it is logical that training deals intensively with the psychological aspect of the customer relationship. 80 percent of those questioned were satisfied with the content and scope of training. Over two thirds felt that their self-confidence in relation to the customer had been increased. One third of those questioned thought that this increase in self-confidence has even had an effect as regards their family life. Beck's training is organised on the basis of two-day seminars which means that there is enough time for all kinds of conflicts to be fully discussed. The seminars give people an opportunity to look again at their own problems, and not just from the departmental viewpoint. Participants are encouraged to solve problems themselves instead of waiting for superiors to find a solution, and it is assumed that they themselves play a part in any relationship problems they may have with superiors, so that they are made aware that they too can affect a conflict. All this follows logically from the notion of the saleswoman as a self-confident and independent host.

Training is also designed to counteract the fact that while the general level of education in society has risen, the level of education in the retail trade continues to be relatively low. The educational qualifications of Beck's staff, with 75 percent having passed the Secondary School Leaving Examinations, 9 percent with the equivalent of GCE 'O' Levels, and 5 percent with GCE 'A' Levels, is close to the average level of education in the retail trade. Further training has enabled the company to ensure that their employees do indeed reflect the clientele, something quite new in the retail trade. Beck's claim to be trend-setting and avant-garde attracts saleswomen and female customers who tend to have a new image of themselves. The customer, easy to get along with and 'free' of conventions and fixations about sterotyped roles, encounters a saleswoman who feels the same way. Many of the saleswomen feel that the fact that they are assigned to the department in which they wish to work, which corresponds to their own conception of themselves, gives them great incentive. A former female student, who works in a department selling exclusive and rather pricy goods, feels it is a great incentive, for instance, to 'be able to raise herself above the average':

One can see immediately from the bearing and deportment of the customers that they come from a good background. I get a great deal of enjoyment from just chatting to them on an educated level, above and beyond sales talk. The fact that the company not only tolerates this, but even expects it, gives me the certainty that I have chosen the right job with the right company.

This is expressed in another way by a young 28-year-old single saleswoman who works in a department selling goods for trend-conscious teenagers:

I like working here. I am well placed to sell goods to "swinging singles" since I am also about the same age, and the customers I deal with have the same outlook. I think it's good that Beck is trying to employ girls who can identify with their customers.

The Beck Department Store: A Case Study

On the other hand, the majority of older saleswomen tend to emphasise the traditional side of the company. Their more maternal way of relating to people appeals to a specific type of middle-class customer. Beck primarily employs two basic types of women who are reflected in the goods on sale. The young, easy-going type and the cultivated, more mature woman. For 35 percent of the employees, Beck's special image was the reason they wanted to work there and, for 25 percent, it was the high-class clientele. The company management considers their new conception of the saleswoman to be highly successful. Productivity has been increased by giving the female employees greater incentives. The company now attracts women whose education and personality would previously never have let them consider working as a saleswoman. If one talks to the women about their chosen profession, all of them say that the crucial factor is having contact and dealing with people. For some of them, working in the sales profession was more or less a logical consequence of their school background, even though some of them would have rather had more school education so that they could have become nurses etc. However, it is still the case that for the majority being a saleswoman was the job which they always wanted. Of course, there are many reasons for this, related to the nature of the labour market, and the overall sexual division of labour within it. The fact that training opportunities for girls are primarily available in service professions, is one decisive factor governing the kind of job girls choose; in 1982 the most popular job was that of saleswoman (Suddeutsche Zeitung, 16.1.1983). The apprenticeship for saleswomen can be for either two or three years. In more and more cases, girls are now opting for the longer, more demanding, three-year apprenticeship.

The fact that so many girls choose a career as a saleswoman should not be seen solely as a negative choice, reflecting their unquestioning acceptance of a traditional female role model. It may also be a positive choice with girls deriving strength and a sense of security from a job for which they feel they have the necessary skills, and which allows them, indeed expects them to express a specifically female personality. The Beck philosophy, quite consciously, continually reinforces the saleswomen's sense of themselves as women. The result of this is not stereotyped shop window dummies who, so to speak, are forced to use their femininity to sell.

The Beck Department Store: A Case Study

Most of the saleswomen in fact define themselves as women not merely in terms of fashion and beauty consciousness, but also in the way they relate to other people. Beck models its notion of the saleswoman on what are often seen as specifically female skills and qualities. The skills and qualities associated with women in general tend to be undervalued in society, and jobs which involve serving people tend to be low-paid; looked at from this point of view, Beck's moves toward creating a positive professional image for saleswoman should be welcomed since they imply an upgrading of the female role in our society; and this is reflected in the saleswomen's pay and conditions at Beck which are significantly better than in other local stores. In the words of a 30-year-old married employee:

> I lead my own life here, have my own contacts and can really be me. Of course, fashion isn't everything, but now and again it is nice to be smartly dressed and to dress someone else smartly. I feel that because I am so accepted as a woman here, I go back to my family with an enormous amount of self-confidence. Although I now have two children and don't need to work for financial reasons, I want to carry on working. My job gives me a great feeling of being a woman and it does me good.

A FAMILY-ORIENTATED ATMOSPHERE MAKES IT EASIER TO RECONCILE THE DEMANDS OF THE FAMILY AND JOB

You have to 'Feel good' in order to 'Sell well'
The world of employment and the world of the family operate according to two rather different kinds of logic, but if there is a family-orientated atmosphere in the workplace, this can have a significant impact on the ability of employees to cope with their two, and sometimes contradictory, identities as both employees and family members. At Beck, over 78 percent of the female employees questioned agreed that the company was sympathetic to family problems and was generous when it comes to doing something for the family. This atmosphere was first created by the paternal and patriarchal style of the late senior partner and has been continued by the present management. In the words of the managing director who was formerly head of the personnel department:

128

It has been fun to experience a caring environment. It simply did one good, even the little things that didn't quite work out as planned. It's all a question of atmosphere. I know it demands a lot to be generous, yet we try here to create this kind of atmosphere; I think it is a question of the quality of life.

This generosity has helped, and continues to help, women at difficult stages of life. For instance, even before the IWT scheme was introduced, if necessary, hours of work could be negotiated individually so that mothers were able to look after their children, similarly employees could be accompanied to the Labour Exchange or Housing Office, and they would also be given assistance during divorce cases. As a result, female employees who have been working with the company for a long time feel as if they are almost part of the family. In the words of a member of the Works Council who has been employed at Beck for many years:

There is a very special atmosphere right from the company management down to the shop floor. The bosses have always taken care of everyone and know all about different individual personal needs and problems. This caring attitude runs right through the company from the top to the bottom and everyone has, at some time, profited from it. This is why we had wage increases even before collectively bargained agreements were introduced, more social welfare benefits and services, and is also why these benefits and services have not only applied to full-timers but equally on a pro rata basis to part-timers. It was not until after the official collectively bargained agreements were reached that we saw how good conditions at Beck actually are.

This caring attitude stems from the belief that how a saleswoman feels is reflected in her sales performance.

'You have to feel good to sell well.' How can a saleswoman feel good if she is obsessed by her own personal worries or if she has no one to look after her children properly during the day, and so on. In other words, we cannot discuss the work situation without talking about the other side of the employee's personality: their life as part of a family. As yet, however, most companies refuse even to discuss the family in the context of the workplace, even though this is the answer to many of the problems involved: not only does an acceptance of the employee's entire personality promote a positive attitude to the company, it also promotes incentive and commitment. As one divorced 35-year-old employee with two school-aged children put it:

> It was the first time that anyone had asked me during an interview whether I had any problems as far as looking after my children was concerned, and it was the first time that anyone told me that if I did have such problems I should tell them and a solution could be found. That gave me such positive incentive to work here and it means that my mind is much clearer to concentrate on other things at work.

Of course, the company also has its own interests at heart; it is important that the investment made in new employees results in employees who, despite their family obligations, are fully able to cope with their job . The key point is that the company is flexible in such a way as to benefit both sides. In individual cases a sympathetic and understanding attitude to family worries is helpful, but it is the general attitude and atmosphere of the company which stresses that family problems, in so far as they affect work can and should be expressed, which is vital. Time and time again, during interviews, women stated that they felt as if they were being treated as people and thought that their family selves were also appreciated. In the words of a department manageress who also has two grown-up children:

> I want my girls to enjoy going to work. Since I consider it a basic right that people be treated as people, it must be possible to talk about family issues from time to time and to share family problems that arise. This little bit of sympathy helps regardless of whether things are going well or badly. I have always been supported by the company and am able to put this into practice because the company policy has always been to retain a little human sympathy.

This is also assisted by the management gesture of thanking the saleswomen on the PA system for a good turnover for instance. Another example is the head of sales who, when things are particularly hectic,

The Beck Department Store: A Case Study

not only works along with the others but also thanks
them and expresses his appreciation.
    Those who put this sympathetic policy into
practice must be sincere, otherwise it remains no
more than a managerial technique. But this also
means that the success or failure of the system is
highly dependent on particular individuals and may
break down if they leave or are transferred. Something of this kind is suggested by the statements
made by some employees who are only willing to work
in specific departments and would hand in their
notice if they were transferred.


The IWT Scheme shows that the Demands of the Workplace and those of the Family should be Seen as
Equal
The different atmospheres of different departments
is reflected in exactly how the IWT scheme operates;
that is, just how far the individual needs of
employees are accommodated. The majority of employees think that the IWT scheme works well,
especially as regards the short-term flexibility
which is so necessary for those with family obligations. Two thirds of those questioned thought that
individual wishes for short-term changes are taken
into consideration (see Table 5.4). However, this is
very dependent upon the department management and,
in particular, on the department manageress who is
responsible for planning where and how personnel are
deployed in her department. Her personal assessment
of the needs of her staff, plus sales targets, are
the crucial factors as regards deploying staff. The
fact that this juggling of competing demands does
not always fully satisfy the staff however, and 46
percent of those questioned thought that it was the
department's needs rather than those of the employee
that tended to take priority. Those departments
where the female employees were satisfied with their
work schedule were those in which the family obligations of individual employees were seen as being
taken into consideration in the planning of individuals' daily work schedules. In the words of a
married part-timer with two children aged ten and
four:

    It is all a question of give and take. Up to
    now, I have always been able to have time off
    when I have needed it. All of us here under-
    stand each other's family demands and problems.
    Of course, I also feel morally obliged to make

131

myself available to the department manageress
the next time she is looking for someone to
stand in for one of my colleagues. She often
has to telephone around her staff until eleven
o'clock in the evening to find a satisfactory
solution. For me it is not so much moral
pressure as a question of loyalty towards my
colleagues.

However well or badly the IWT scheme works in the
day-to-day reality of different departments, it has
created something quite new in the working world:
it has shown that it is possible for the obligations
staff have towards their families, as well as those
they have as employees, to be recognised as equally
important. Family obligations which spill over into
work time can be accommodated when individuals' work
schedules are drawn up; and this happens not simply
on an informal level, organised through personal
relationships, but is built into the official structure of the company.

**It is not True that Full-timers Identify with their
Job while Part-timers Identify with their Family**
Does Beck, by creating flexible opportunities for
part-time work, meet the needs of women to find a
'successful form of coping with professional and
family demand'? (Eckart, 1982:25). Or is it merely
the only option available to certain women because
of their domestic work commitments within the
family? To see it this way would mean that part-time
work would be considered as only 'half going out to
work', that is half emancipation, whilst 'full'
emancipation can only be achieved by working full-
time. This definition of part-time work is not only
dangerous but also false since it reinforces the way
women are torn between the public and private sphere
whereby, depending upon the needs of labour-market
at any one time, women are either propelled out of
the house or pushed back into it.
In our survey at Beck, 56 percent were part-
timers and 44 percent full-timers. When we asked
the part-timers why, apart from financial reasons,
they have opted for part-time, 58 percent said it
was so that they would be able to combine family
obligations with those of the workplace more satis-
factorily, 46 percent said that they did not want to
devote all their energies to work and wanted to save
some for themselves, and 37 percent said that it was
for health reasons. A statement made by a 45-year-

old married part-timer with three children is representative of many:

> I needed something else in my life apart from
> my husband and my housework. After all, a
> woman cannot only exist through washing nappies
> and always being there for the children and her
> husband. We women want something more out of
> life, we want to experience it fully, and it's
> that experience that I get here.

All women, whether they work full-time or part-time,
stated that the main reason they work is financial.
83 percent of the married women contributed to the
common household budget. Yet their financial independence and the autonomy associated with this were
also important motives.

71 percent of all women state that they want to
be with other people, not just within a private
sphere of family and personal life, but in a public-
ly recognised work environment. The isolation of the
nuclear family and society's underestimation of
domestic and reproductive work are significant here.

In addition to developing their identity as
socially recognised employees, women also want to
have the opportunity to develop their identities
within the family. One important reason for working
part-time is so that it is possible to perform the
necessary tasks within the family and not be under
constant stress, 'both aspects need to be given due
consideration.' Thus, twice as many full-time as
part-time employees said they found combining family
and working life as 'very difficult or difficult'.
39 percent of full-timers and only 16 percent of
part-timers consider the 'distance' from the family
to be negative. One female employee, married with
two children who has worked for many years, compared
her previous full-time work with her present part-
time work as follows:

> When I was working full-time, I could not allow
> myself to put anything off, or delay anything,
> since I always had a full schedule. Today, I
> cannot understand how I managed everything; the
> quality of my life has now improved enormously.
> I really like going to work every day. Some-
> times I'm really glad to get there, I'm looking
> forward to seeing my colleagues and to doing my
> work. But that doesn't mean that I am not
> equally as glad when I'm back home. I have been
> able to strike a good balance and to experience

133

both dimensions.

There is little evidence that women who work full-time receive substantially more assistance from their husbands or partners as regards household chores etc. Rather, assistance is characterised by qualitative differences, regardless of whether a woman works full-time or part-time. Depending upon the particular pattern established within the individual family, the husband or partner undertakes various tasks such as shopping, cooking, washing and cleaning. Yet more important than the activity itself is the acknowledgement of the importance of such tasks which is signified to women by the very fact that their husbands help with them. At some level, women associate this help with an acknowledgement of the importance of the domestic role of women. But male trespassing onto the female domain is not always welcomed; some women prefer clearly defined spheres of responsibility. As one 50-year-old married full-timer put it:

> I find that when my husband helps me it is more of a hindrance. When he does something he is all fingers and thumbs, but he always thinks he can do it better than I can and criticises me whatever I do. That's why I would rather do everything in my own way. He does all the repairs and I leave them to him.

This is where not only two different work rhythms, but two differently acquired types of logic clash. As ideal types, housework is opposed to the world of employment. The job, because it is embedded in a developed and market-orientated economic order, requires more than simply a practical training. Competition, rational thinking and the will to succeed are not only cliches of male behaviour patterns, but are also a particular pattern of behaviour deriving from, and acquired in a profit-orientated society geared to production. Conversely, housework, and in a broader sense reproduction work, necessitates empathy, patience, perseverance, and knowledge gained by experience and divergent thinking. These differing behavioural patterns - polarised in man and woman - are reflected in male and female cultures. Because we live in a male-dominated society, the demand simply for formal equality between men and women would lead in fact to a negation of female logic and an acceptance of the hegemony of male logic.

# The Beck Department Store: A Case Study

There may be a number of different reasons why women who work part-time tend to be less satisfied with the help their husbands give them as regards household chores than full-timers. It may be related to the fact that many women who have reduced their working hours have become more demanding:

> I find that with my children the part-time work which I do today almost more of a burden than when I was working full-time. Before, I looked on the stress I felt differently, simply because I didn't have a chance of changing things, I just had to manage somehow. I now allow myself to think of my own needs and I seem to feel the stress more. I have more freedom and I am more aware.

This time for oneself and the fact that part-timers feel happier and have more energy than full-timers also means that part-timers have a generally richer life. Thus, part-timers were more often satisfied with the time they spent with their partner than is the case with those who work full-time. Yet they also expect more from their husband. They not only want him to help more with household chores but they also want him to assume greater responsibility as regards bringing up the children.

Virtually 60 percent of those who previously worked full-time, and now work part-time, feel that they now have a greater commitment to their job. The sense of having more freedom makes dealing with customers more enjoyable and indirectly boosts their sales performance. They find their work situation more pleasant than full-timers. For them the change between the rhythm of the workplace and the rhythm of home is crucial. To know that tomorrow they will be able to have a rest at home, stimulates them to put more effort into their work.

The majority of those working full-time disassociate themselves in certain respects from the part-timers. For instance, they believe that they know more about their stock. However, only some part-time workers would agree with this. In the words of one part-timer:

> It is completely up to me as to what effort I put in, whether I myself bother to note, for instance, what goods have arrived and how I am to sell them. Perhaps I should make more of an effort to obtain information on collections etc. But it is all a question of personal

commitment, a question of what I want from the job and not a question of how I work. People differ everywhere and it is more a question of an individual's personal attitude to work.

Part-timers and full-timers were in almost full agreement as regards their career prospects. Both groups considered that full-timers have much greater opportunities in terms of promotion and part-timers see themselves as being excluded from promotion possibilities. In actual fact, we should rather see the career progress of part-timers the other way round: while it is possible for a department manageress to reduce her working time, a part-timer cannot become a department manageress.

This reflects a deep-rooted prejudice against part-timers; 'part-time work' is taken to mean no more than partial commitment. The Managing Director had, and still has, to break down this prejudice even amongst his own managerial staff. Part-timers still have to choose between either a career or a better balance between their job and family. This fact, which is accepted as a basic reality, is reflected in that they also know the different career perspectives of women who work part-time, only 4 percent of whom want to have a career as compared with 18 percent of women who work full-time. This has far-reaching consequences; for example, it makes the prospect of having a job far less attractive in general for those whose family responsibilities prevent them working full-time, and means that their job is almost always seen as less important than that of their husbands, so that when family decisions are taken on job changes, the employed husband necessarily always takes priority.

Even integration into the department is perceived differently. While half of all those questioned believed that integration is not related to the number of hours worked, most of the full-timers considered that their part-time colleagues have less chance to integrate themselves in the department simply because they are there less time.

Some degree of competition between full-timers and part-timers can be detected. Yet not in the sense that might have been anticipated of full commitment versus partial commitment. Part-time work which our society devalues has become the more desirable option in this case. There seems to be some envy of what is perceived as the advantageous position of the married women, who can 'afford' to work part-time. This statement appears to be more

The Beck Department Store: A Case Study

significant than the often assumed differing levels
of commitment of part-timers and full-timers. The
younger, single full-timers are necessarily geared
more intensely to their jobs. Yet since they are
sole earners in the majority of cases, they are
clearly less happy with their financial situation
than are their part-time colleagues. The fact that
45 percent of all full-timers would like to work
part-time if they had the choice clearly indicates a
desire for the improved quality of life which working part-time allows if this is possible financially.

SIGNIFICANCE OF THE LIFE CYCLE,
SUBJECTIVE PERSPECTIVES OF FAMILY AND JOB

'Free and Unattached' - yet Life isn't a great deal
easier.
12 percent (all full-timers) of all those questioned thought that combining job and family is
particularly difficult. Most of this group are over
38 years old and tended to be living without a
partner, and work full-time. They considered the
standard working hours of the retail trade to be the
greatest constraint on their private life. Working
173 hours per month, and working Saturdays, gives
them little chance to spend time with their friends
and acquaintances. During the week the pressures of
their job leave them too exhausted to do more than a
minimum of housework. It is noticeable that they
tend to have a very regulated and well-planned
routine of household chores, even on their day-off.
Admittedly, this planning gives them a sense of
security, but it also tends to make them feel as if
they are permanently tied down. The majority of them
have organised their lives so that they no longer
have the energy to establish or maintain a lasting
relationship, and frequently do not see the need for
such a relationship. In the words of one 30-year-old
employee who has been divorced for six years:

> Now that I have learnt to stand on my own feet,
> I do not intend to become dependent again. I
> can take care of myself and that has been my
> most important experience. If there was a man
> around I would not be able to organise my
> evenings the way I do. I would be constrained,
> would have to give up a great deal and I say to
> myself - why should I?

# The Beck Department Store: A Case Study

The job of selling depends to a large extent on communication, and it is this aspect of their job that gives them the most satisfaction and feeling of being in the right job. They consider the challenge of the job to have the greatest positive effect on their private lives. The special image which Beck cultivates, upgrades their identity as saleswomen. The deliberately fostered female culture at Beck - they tend to socialise with colleagues in a similar situation in their free time - gives them a sense of having a full social identity. The communication aspect of their job, however, also has other effects: stress, mental exhaustion and, during peak periods, the feeling that 'they don't want to say a word in the evening.' While the saleswomen cultivate various relationships, these kinds of feelings often mean that they are no longer prepared to summon up the energy for arguments, or to make the effort to adapt to different lives. Some of them have children who are already grown-up so that they no longer feel overburdened by their maternal role, rather they enjoy the achievements of their children, whether this has been in the job or marriage stakes. The IWT scheme has important effects on the private lives of employees with the large majority (63 percent of those questioned), seeing IWT as having positive benefits as far as personal and family life is concerned, and only 16 percent seeing it as having negative effects. Even though they have less flexibility in terms of free time, full-timers as well as part-timers valued the flexibility the scheme gives them. In the words of a single, 40-year-old full-timer:

> It's just great. If I want to have a cup of coffee outside breaktime or longer than the usual breaktime, or if I want to meet someone briefly, there is no need for a lot of fuss or having to ask loads of people, and that is very important to me. Admittedly, I don't have a great deal of leeway, yet I can make my own decisions, and that little bit of independence should not be underestimated. You wouldn't believe how valuable it is.

It is the legal restrictions governing the hours of full-timers - the result of collective bargaining between the unions and management - and covering the retail trade as a whole - that curtails the amount of flexibility IWT can offer full-timers. Admittedly, the IWT scheme is designed so that the overtime

138

worked, or hours owing, do not need to be balanced up until the end of the year even though the individual's salary remains the same each month, but nevertheless, full-timers have less scope to juggle with their hours because of the legislation. If a part-timer has a considerable number of hours to make up, she is able to make these up by working on one of her days off, but a full-timer cannot do this because it is legally stipulated that she must have a day off. The electronic measurement of the exact time worked by each employee was considered to be fair by 90 percent of respondents and it means that everybody can see at a glance whether they are in credit or deficit as regards hours worked. The majority of all full-timers, whether single or married, see it is a problem when they owe hours to the company, but at the same time they feel that it is important that whether or not an individual goes into deficit is decided at least to a certain extent by that individual themselves and not simply by management. Other disadvantages of IWT cited were the flexibility it gives to management so that, for instance, staff are not always sure if they will get the hours off in the evening that they want, since this is dependent on the course of business during the day. Similarly, any time they take off is recorded, there are no unofficial breaks. Being in deficit affects different employees in different ways: 'I desperately try to keep my hours and I do not for instance enjoy shopping during regular working time since I find it causes me more stress to know that I have to make the time up again.' It affects others less:

> For me it is not so much of a burden as I have until the end of the year to make the hours up. This also suits the company, since it is at the end of the year - that is at Christmas time - when I make up the hours and that is the time when things are chaotic and there is always enough work to go round.

Despite some criticisms, by and large all full-timers are in favour of the IWT scheme. 40 percent of those questioned said that the greater sense of independence it gives them as a result of allowing them a say, even if it is a small say, in exactly what hours they work is a great advantage. Admittedly, the full-timers feel that the idea of flexibility operates more in the case of part-timers than it does for full-timers, but they too want greater flexibility; and the fact that there now exists the possibility of some kind of say as regards work schedules has in itself created the desire to exercise this right. For the majority of full-timers, financial constraints are the reason why they cannot work part-time and take fuller advantage of the IWT scheme. It was clear from our interviews that if they were able to reduce their working hours by 10 to 30 hours per month, this could lessen their basic sense of being overburdened. They feel that a reduction like this in their working hours would also benefit their sales performance since one has to 'feel good' in order to 'sell well.' By this they also saw their job as an essential part of their life and defined themselves as identifying predomi-nantly with their job and as deriving a lot of mental energy from this.

Understandably, many of the older saleswomen in particular would like to reduce their hours in the time leading up to their retirement, but because pensions are calculated on the basis of the last ten working years they are forced to 'stick it out' in order to be able to claim a full pension. Some older, single women employees do accept · a lower pension, reducing their hours slightly, so as to prepare themselves better for the transition to full retirement.

All the younger, married women who were interviewed and who work full-time hope to be able to work part-time after the birth of their first child. The possibility that Beck gives them of being able to continue to work part-time prevents them from feeling that they have to make the classic choice between work and children. The reasons for not having a child for the time being tend to be to do with wanting to be able to contribute financially to setting up the household and enjoying a period of freedom before becoming a parent at a later date. They still feel youthful and do not think the burden of balancing work and personal relationships is a serious one. They are also less afraid of conflict and are ready to demand that household chores are shared. Consequently they do not find it necessary to work fewer hours in order to cope with their domestic tasks. As yet their job provides them with positive rewards in terms of mental energy and stress in fairly equal measure.

The Worst Off: Single Mothers who Work Full-time
While it is the young, married saleswomen who seem

to have least problems as regards combining a job and family,. it is single mothers who work full-time who are in the worst position. There were not many in our sample, yet those we did find were both very committed saleswomen and also highly responsible mothers. There is one thing they find impossible, however, to enter into a lasting relationship. In the words of a 35-year-old mother of two adolescent children:

> I would love to have a boyfriend, but without firm ties. I still manage to have a good relationship with my children and I can cope with the inevitable arguments, but I would no longer be able to do that if I had a man or a husband. I am not bitter about it, it is just that there is a limit to what I can do and I had to make a decision: either children or a relationship.

The typical schedule of a normal, ordinary day for such a woman is the following:

1. Up at 6.00 a.m., maybe finish preparing the children's midday meal, cooked the evening before.
2. 7.00 a.m., breakfast with the children, possibly checking the children's homework done the night before in between having coffee at breakfast, writing a shopping list.
3. 8.00 a.m. off to work.
4. 8.30 a.m., start work: smartly dressed, wide-awake and friendly: in between, calling home to find out whether the children enjoyed the pre-cooked meal, possibly adding things to the shopping list (the children do the shopping), asking what the children are doing in the afternoon.
5. 6.30 p.m., finish work.
6. 7.00 p.m., arrive back home.
7. 7.00 p.m. to 8.00 p.m., evening meal with the children, discussing problems at school, settling an argument between the brothers and sisters and telling the children what happened at work.
8. 8.00 p.m. to 10.00 p.m., preparing the meal for the following day, doing the washing, ironing, patching and darning clothes, doing the family's paperwork, settling bills, filling in school forms etc.
9. 10.00 p.m. to 11.00 p.m., either knitting,

watching television, reading or sleeping.
10. After 11.00 p.m., time to go to bed.

Although the children are responsible for certain household tasks which makes things easier for their mother, nevertheless she still has to ring home now and again to check that everything has been done, to listen to how the children are getting on, and whether there are problems at school, or a quarrel. Because they work on Saturdays, Beck saleswomen get a day off in lieu during the week; for those who are single parents this day is normally taken up with cleaning the house, major weekly shopping and so forth. This only leaves Saturday evening and Sunday free, either for a trip somewhere with the children, a chat with a friend or simply just being at home. Where do mothers such as these find the energy to cope with their punishing schedule?

> The feeling of working full-time - I have to do it because of the money: we have little enough and I have to count every penny because there really isn't enough to go round - does, however, give me a feeling of self-confidence. I might even say a new awareness of life. My work revives me, I get a great feeling that I am doing the right thing and come home with new strength. On the other hand, my life is also centred around guiding my teenage children and watching them become adults, and I am proud that we do manage.

Not every woman in the same situation is so optimistic and full of life, yet they all have two things in common: the feeling that they are doing the right thing and a self-confidence, derived from their jobs, that this helps them in bringing up their children. This confidence plays an important role in counterbalancing their feelings of guilt about not spending enough time with their children, not being able to give them the help they need with their school work, and sometimes because they, the mothers, are under such pressure, being short-tempered. Yet they also see the fact that they work as having positive effects on their children; for instance, they feel it is good for children, particularly boys, to do some housework, and they hoped that they are giving their children a positive image of women in general - even if they themselves sometimes have moments of weakness. All of them have sacrificed any hope they might have had for a career of their own for the sake of their children. Above all, this is because of the extra time demands a career would make, which would leave them even less time for their children. Neither their sacrifices nor their considerable achievement in managing their double burden of job and children, however, is rewarded in modern industrial society, which makes the IWT scheme all the more important for women bringing up children on their own. It not only helps them practically to organise their time in the most efficient ways, but it also helps them cope mentally more easily with their job and home. But they had to learn to muster the self confidence to talk about their family problems at work as well:

> At first I didn't want to say anything in the department about the problems I have at home. But one day when I was phoned at work to be told that my child had hurt himself, I was sent straight home to comfort him and take care of him. Of course, I had to make the time up: you never get anything for nothing. But you always have the feeling that they will give you time off if it's really necessary and that feeling is worth more than anything else in the world. It doesn't just have to be a child hurting themselves, it could also be a quarrel, or even one of your children visiting you. When I take time off, I don't have a sense of obligation and I don't need to crawl to other people and thank them, it is my right to have time off when I want it. That is what makes me more and more self-confident about being able to reconcile my family and my job and not having to keep them separate.

This self-confidence can only flourish in departments in which the managers are fully behind the idea of IWT, so that it really does become 'individual' worktime. One young department manager who trained at Beck said this:

> I have already seen how IWT can be completely distorted by excessive regimentation and supervision. What I find is that I must give people a certain degree of freedom and the feeling that they are trusted; in doing this I need to consider what motivates me, what I myself would do in a specific situation etc., and that is

143

how I must treat others. Since I only work with
women here, it is quite natural for me to talk
to them about family matters. I think that IWT
is not only a good solution for women, it also
encourages people to take account of the family
dimension in a more general sense.

The single parents at Beck were very grateful for
the flexibility IWT gives them; in general, those in
this situation have such a difficult time because
of the prejudice with which society views them that
they tend simply to be thankful for anything that
makes life a little easier for them, rather than
feeling they are in a position to make any demands
themselves. However, their maternal role not only
takes up a great deal of energy, it also gives them
back a great deal of energy and vigour. This seems
to be the difference between them and single full-
timers who often seem to feel, subjectively, under
greater stress. As well as their jobs, these mothers
have another important task, that of guiding their
children into adulthood and simply being there with
their children. This has an important effect on how
they see their job. For this group of women, who are
bringing up children on their own, the ideal solution would be to work part-time, with the same or
even higher wage, so that they would not continually
have to lead such a hand-to-mouth existence.

Many full-time female employees want to be able
to work less hours for the same pay, regardless of
the stage of life they are at; changes such as
finishing earlier in the evening or, above all,
having to work less hours on Saturdays (even if it
were only a restriction in the summer months or a
general reduction of Saturday work) would, they
felt, significantly improve their private or family
life. It would also slightly reduce the stress
caused by the often difficult physical working
conditions such as the stuffy atmosphere, lighting
conditions and having to stand all day.


Mothers with Small Children:
It Works if you have a Granny
Is IWT the ideal solution for women who have a
family and work part-time? We must differentiate
here according to the age of the children. Very few
(6 percent) of those questioned were women aged 28
or less who were married with children under 10 and
who worked part-time. The reason for this is the
particular nature of the IWT scheme and the hours of

The Beck Department Store: A Case Study

State childcare facilities and schools.
The IWT scheme is based on a maximum level of staffing from 11.00 a.m. to approximately 2.00 p.m., and then again from 4.00 p.m. to 6.00 p.m. Creche opening times are from 7.00 a.m. to 5.00 p.m., and those of the Kindergarten from 7.00 a.m. to midday, and then again from 2.00 p.m. to 5.00 p.m. School hours are generally from 8.00 a.m. to 1.00 p.m. This means that the times employees need to be at work are often precisely those when they really need to be at home or when they have to fetch their children.

The work schedules of Beck's employees are individually negotiated and represent a compromise between interests of the company and the interests of the employees. This means an employee might work from 10.00 a.m. to 3.00 p.m. or 8.30 a.m. to 4.00 p.m. daily, or possibly three full consecutive days every week, or work alternate days. A whole host of different work schedules are feasible, yet they all have one thing in common: times during which there are a large number of customers cannot be exchanged at will for work times during which there are few customers. In individual cases, a solution may be found by moving someone from another department, but possibilities are limited. Only when their children have reached a certain age can mothers fit in with these constraints. This also explains why there are a high percentage (over 70 percent) of women aged between 38 and 60 who work part-time.

Those part-timers who are mothers with small children have usually solved the problem of looking after the children by enlisting the help of the children's grandmothers. Depending upon the age of the children, some of them are also looked after in a Kindergarten for a few hours. All such part-timers have one thing in common: they have found a good balance as regards combining job and family, and this affects their overall assessment of their job situation: 80 percent of them said it had been satisfactory during the last few months. Given the many, and often conflicting obligations such women have, such a positive assessment can only be understood if their family situation is taken into account. One woman who has two children, one school-age and one younger, is typical of many:

> I have found a good balance thanks to working part-time. I enjoy going to work, and this puts the everyday little upsets and problems in a different perspective. When I am at home, I

145

> devote myself entirely to the children. For
> instance, I work two whole days, yet never
> consecutively, and two short Saturdays. I do
> not start until 10.00 a.m. and this is very
> important to me as regards the quality of life
> I have with my children. It means I have the
> time to sit down and have breakfast with them,
> take the youngest to the Kindergarten, while
> still having time to do the necessary household
> chores. My mother and father-in-law look after
> my children until my husband comes home. After
> I have worked one day, before going to work
> again, I have a day in between to do something
> with my children. I feel that I am stretched to
> the full in both aspects of my life, my job and
> my family, but I am also very satisfied.

Other female employees prefer a block working time
of two to three consecutive days. Particularly when
the children are still toddlers, they see the advantage of being able to look after them constantly for
two or three days at a time.

These part-timers describe their work situation
as being ideal. It gives them the mental space they
need to prevent them from feeling overwhelmed by
their maternal role. At the same time they leave no
doubt that they want to be able to enjoy the
maternal dimension of their lives, and indeed it was
this that made them decide to work part-time so that
they could combine both. Whether, as in the case of
younger mothers, it is that they do not want to lose
touch with the world of employment, even if their
career prospects are limited, or whether they just
want to experience something else after having
worked for a long period, there is a clear desire to
have a job and a satisfying family life. In the
words of a 36-year-old part-timer, a mother with a
2-year-old child: 'I really enjoyed my job, but I
didn't want to carve out a career for myself because
I realised that a job is not all there is in life.'

Dependent upon the physical and mental stress,
these mothers experience a new job motivation when
they return to work after maternity leave, and their
job means something rather different to them than it
did before they had their child:

> Here I can talk about different things and
> occupy my time in other ways. For me, work has
> now become the place where I can make a good
> job of something which, because of my child, I
> never manage to do at home now. All this gives

me the energy at work. Being at home gives me a
completely different kind of energy because I
have the important emotional bond with my
child.

It is precisely the flexibility afforded them by the
IWT scheme that relieves some of the mental stress
they experience as a result of having to succeed in
two roles: that of mother and of working woman. In
the words of a part-timer with a child aged 18
months:

> Admittedly, I do try to keep to the agreed
> times of my work schedule, but I can still find
> time to give my child that little extra kiss in
> the morning and I don't feel under pressure.
> This little bit of freedom is very important
> for me, particularly in terms of incentive
> while I am at work so that my mind is free to
> concentrate on my work. The good atmosphere in
> my department means that I can usually find
> someone who will help me out if I want to swap
> because of my child.

Sacrificing one's own interests for the sake of a
colleague in the department may stretch the basic
concept of give and take. However, what exactly
constitutes an acceptable demand is always highly
subjective. In a more rigid department, this may
even extend to insisting that someone stands in for
a colleague. In other, more flexible, departments
staff may not even be prepared to work voluntarily
on a Saturday in order to increase department turnover.
  Often mothers with small children do not even
have to make the decision when they are faced with a
'swap situation', as their colleagues with older
children will volunteer to stand in for them since
they usually find it easier to reorganise their
work time. Mutual assistance tends to operate
smoothly when the employees in a particular department have different sets of family obligations. If
all employees were to be in a similar family situation, mothers with small children say, the scope
for flexibility would rapidly be exhausted and conflict would become more likely. Those who have the
most flexibility are the part-timers with older
children. Part-timers are always expected to be
more flexible since they have a much greater range
of possible work schedules generally. This is also
the reason why they feel greater stress than full-

timers when they are in deficit with their hours. How does this group of part-timers, aged between 38 and 60 who make over 70 percent of the part-time staff, feel about their job and family situations?

## Middle-aged Mothers:
### Satisfied yet under Great Stress

All the women in this category have one thing in common: they started working again, after being housewives for ranging lengths of time, after their children were born. Above all, they got a job to escape their isolation. The popular stereotype is of the loving, selfless mother who is always there and does everything she is supposed to do within the cloistered world of the nuclear family. They themselves recognise their need for contact, and social recognition cannot be satisfied simply through their children, they also want to participate in a more public world. 70 percent of those questioned thought that it was their paid employment which gave them greater social recognition. They are also conscious of the danger of becoming blinkered as to the wider world if their life is totally confined' to the domestic sphere. But they also feel that the stereotype of the full-time employee has its own set of blinkers. Over half of the part-timers thought that most people work too much and have too little time for the other important things in life. They try to put into practice their feeling that this excessive concentration on work can also have a bad effect on family life and that, therefore, the family must not be simply dismissed as being of little importance, and they feel that they are able to do this more than full-timers. In this respect they want to escape from the straight-jacket of the old stereotype of the working housewife. They see themselves very much as employees and are determined to maintain this part of their identity within the family context come what may. A part-timer with three children expressed it like this:

I certainly had to argue with my husband about my job, I would even go so far as to say I had to fight to go back to work. My husband considers that it is quite natural for me to stay home with the children. As they got a bit older, I would almost say I fled to my job. I looked for a part-time job since this was the only way I could cope with everything. On the days when I am at home, I now feel that I have a little more time for myself. It is only now that ' my husband has come to understand what it means to me to have freed myself from the feeling that I ought to be a perfect housewife and mother. Because I work, things don't always work out completely smoothly at home anymore. Yet my job has given me a second identity and, because of this, I feel far more balanced. Today I have two sorts of responsibilities which, admittedly, is a burden, but both of these responsibilities bring me benefits.

For those who have resumed work, after a period at home, there is a shift in the whole dynamic of family life. The mothers consider it more natural to encourage the children , particularly their sons, to help them in the home. They have learnt to stand up for themselves in relation to their children and their husband, and they hope that the way they are living may make it easier for their children:

I had to fight both with myself and my husband to be able to go out to work. I hope that my sons and daughters will not have to struggle as much: husband and wife should share the tasks of being the breadwinner and running a home.

Their self-confidence is very important for them at that very difficult stage when their children reach puberty, helping them to let them make the break from dependence to independence. They feel that it is easier for them than for mothers who are at home all day to, as it were, 'let go'. But at the same time they also worry that because they are working, they may not be giving their children all the guidance they need to prepare them for later life. Both full-timers and part-timers have similar feelings of guilt, even if these feelings are stronger in full-timers:

1. Not providing enough assistance as regards school
2. Not having enough time to talk to each other
3. Not being able to recognise bad influences early so that they can do something about them

Whether they have a partner or live alone, the Beck saleswomen see the time when their children are adolescent as the most critical phase as regards combining a job and family. Some of them even give this as a reason for deciding not to have children. The IWT scheme makes things a lot easier, but it is primarily the part-timers who are able to take advantage of it. One part-timer, a mother with two adolescent children, said this:

> Thanks to the fact that I am able to select my working time to suit my needs, I work Mondays, Thursdays, Fridays and Saturdays, I can be at home for two full days. When I am at home I can concentrate better on my children's problems at school, see my friends or simply help to make the house seem more of a home. It helps a lot to be able to swap working time if I need to because my children need help with homework or if something out of the ordinary crops up.

This is the positive side of the considerable flexibility available to these part-timers. They want to fulfil their responsibilities to their children, and thus it is important to them, and rightly so, that they are able to react spontaneously to the needs of their family. Their job, too, particularly as far as dealing with customers is concerned, is also characterised by the need to be able to cope with unforeseen problems. Many women feel themselves to be highly dependent upon there being the right atmosphere of mutual give and take within their department. Different departments, depending on the particular style adopted by their managers, differ considerably in this respect, and this kind of variation is an important factor in explaining the varying levels of satisfaction with the flexibility of the IWT scheme. But none the less, in general the IWT scheme, in relieving some of the pressure of having to conform to a particular work schedule, has had an important and positive effect on the private lives of the Beck employees. The IWT scheme shows the importance of a degree of flexibility in work schedules for those trying to combine a job with bringing up a family, but it also shows how other needs begin to be articulated once the overwhelming burden of a rigid work schedule is eased slightly. This is also reflected in the weekly schedules of part-timers who have more time for themselves, and to spend with friends and neighbours. A fairly representative example would be:

Monday        Working all day from 8.30 a.m. to

|            | 6.30 p.m., in the evening only doing those household chores that are absolutely necessary (e.g. preparing the meal for the next day, washing the dishes etc.). |
|------------|---|
| Tuesday    | Also working all day, a similar schedule in the evening. |
| Wednesday  | Day off, catching up with the housework of the last two days in the morning, possibly washing and ironing, having a proper midday meal with the children who only ate pre-cooked food the two days before. Afternoon deliberately set aside for relaxation or some kind of leisure activity - doing something with the children or getting together with friends and neighbours for a chat and a cup of coffee, and so on. |
| Thursday   | Day off, doing the main shopping for the week in the morning, having a midday meal with the children, afternoon spent on social activities such as visiting etc., or simply lazing around at home and pursuing one's own interests, finishing off all the other little household chores remaining. |
| Friday     | Working all day. |
| Saturday   | Day off. |
| Sunday     | Day off. |

When assessing such a weekly schedule, it is crucial to establish what importance is attached to the social activities. Is it merely a consolidation of the 'typical female role' relationships? Or is it not really an expression of the desire to experience and put into practice the solidarity and harmony of work, caring for others and being able to structure one's own life as one wishes? Is it the part-timers who are happiest with the balance they have achieved between their family and their job? On the one hand, they feel that the company takes them seriously as employees with certain skills and they feel that they are encouraged to develop themselves as people. The IWT scheme gives them the feeling that their family and its needs is recognised as important, even within the workplace. This recognition, and the actual way the scheme operates, enables a more satisfactory balancing of the respective obligations

of job and family. On the other hand, the stress on
the importance of female experience and female
culture at Beck gives them greater self-confidence
in themselves as women. In this respect, the statements made by the majority of women interviewed
established that they are quite satisfied with their
life as it is at present.

## EMPLOYER INTEREST VERSUS EMPLOYEE INTERESTS

According to one of the magazines to be found in
most managers' offices, there are eight rules for a
successful company (<u>Manager Magazine</u>, June 1983). A
concern with the family life of employees is not one
of them. Success is gauged solely in terms of productivity. These eight rules listed are:

1. Company autonomy.
2. Dynamism.
3. Structures that encourage employees to
   improve their productivity.
4. Simple organisational structure.
5. Receptivity to customer demand.
6. A positive company philosophy.
7. Flexible but disciplined management.
8. A clear company identity.

Despite the fact that the Beck philosophy of recog-
nising and giving importance to the family dimension
of its employees' lives may be somewhat heretical
according to standard management policy; in just
over ten years Beck has managed to double its turnover to over DM 100 million. Average turnover in the
retail trade is approximately DM 8,700 per square
metre, at Beck it is slightly more than DM 10,000
per square metre; and whereas the average turnover
per full-time employee is approximately DM 155,000
per annum, at Beck it is approximately DM 204,000.
    The Managing Director explains these above
average figures as being the result of the company's
respect for the entire personality of its employees
and creating an atmosphere of openness and trust,
together with granting people a certain degree of
freedom. But if this simply becomes a management
technique which is learnt and implemented mechanic-
ally, then it remains lacking in its most important
dimension: being sincere as a person and accepting
all the positive and negative aspects this involves.
This sincerity means being able to accept the emotional dimension, even though this may contradict

the rational work logic. Yet this emotionality also means there being and having to accept a certain amount of conflict and friction; such an attitude, however, also guards against employees being seen too one-sidedly merely as cogs with a certain specific function in the work mechanism. The Managing Director claims to have raised this concept to the level of a philosophy: 'There must be no schizophrenic separation of work and private life. When I work, I am still an entire person and it must be enjoyable. The conditions then must be such that this entire person can also be an "entire person" at work'.

This is reflected in the stress on the family within the company which results from the fact that the majority of its employees are women. This attitude also lies behind Beck's own creation of IWT. If IWT had been implemented only with the aim of improving productivity and efficiency, other flexitime schemes, which are now common in the retail trade, could solely have been introduced. Such schemes are designed solely around maximising employee availability to management so that, for instance, employees are expected to keep themselves in readiness to report for work, sometimes at an hour's notice, whenever their employer decides they are needed. Systems like these have been aptly termed the call-girl system, and are in marked contrast to the very different concern for (and accommodation to) the complicated lives of many women which is such an important feature of Beck's IWT scheme. In the words of the Managing Director:

> For me, a working world organised more in tune with the situation of women means maximum possible flexibility. By this I mean flexibility for both sides, on the part of the employer and one the part of the employee. Before introducing IWT, the company employed economists to look for suitable pre-existing models, but they only found the so-called "call-girl system" which was unacceptable to us. For me it was essential that there was no compulsion in our scheme, it was important to maintain a combination of profit and a constant sales presence, and the only problem was finding the required degree of flexibility. We were virtually forced to "hand-knit" something ourselves. This "hand-knitted" scheme was elaborated with our employers on the basis of existing rigid part-time work arrangement at

Beck, but with the aim of increasing flexibility. It was necessary for the company to
increase its flexibility if it was to make best
use of its staff and organise things so that
the level of staffing would mirror more or less
exactly customer demand with fewer staff, for
instance, not only at slack times of the year,
but during the slack periods that are a regular
part of the shop's daily rhythm. By doing this
the company ensures that its personnel costs
are kept to a minimum, with exactly the right
number of staff being available at any one
time.

But how far is the need to minimise the workforce
compatible with Beck's policy of treating their
employees as whole people? It is clearly important
that the positive benefits of IWT are not eroded
through an excessive work load. From the company's
point of view, if the pressure on employees becomes
too great due to a reduction in the number of staff,
this may impair the level of service saleswomen are
able to give customers, and the level of service at
Beck is something the company prides itself on. The
successful working of the IWT scheme depends on the
co-operation and enthusiasm of employees, and, if in
the interest of productivity, the staff/customer
ratio were reduced too much, this could upset the
delicate balance between the interests of the
employee and of management and cause employees to
lose faith in the scheme.

The crucial point is how much freedom the top
management allows the personnel department in terms
of the approximate planning of staffing levels and
how much leeway the departmental manageresses have
as far as the precise deployment of staff is concerned. This is because it is precisely the departmental manageress who must negotiate the compromise
between the demand to use staff in the most 'efficient' way and the personal interest of her employees. The manageresses, therefore, are central to the
whole operation of IWT. We need to consider how they
see things and what their personal level of commitment is, since both of these affect the kind of
compromises that are achieved. However, they are
also the group subject to the most stress since they
represent the point at which the conflicts between
the different interests of the employer and employee
are fought out. Nevertheless, of the female employees questioned, 28 percent stated that they considered their interest to be best represented by the

departmental manageress and 16 percent by the
personnel management. But 57 percent of all those
questioned thought that they themselves best represented their own interests. This may be one of the
results of Beck's stress on the specificity of the
individual which, on the one hand, affords the
possibility of seeing the individual in the totality
of their particular life situation and not just as
an employee. A formal increase in the respect given
to the individual also brings with it a greater
feeling of autonomy and self-determination. Group
consciousness, on the other hand, is not so promi-
nent and conditions generally at Beck are such that
the employees tend to feel relatively well off;
social welfare services rated by part-timers second,
and by full-timers third, in terms of benefit to
their private lives. Only 12 percent thought that
their interests at Beck were represented by the
works council and, only 2 percent by the trade
union. A 25-year-old full-timer said this:

> I don't see how we could improve the situation
> much. We have so many social welfare benefits
> which people working at other companies can
> only dream of. I think it is more important to
> have enough courage to solve conflicts on the
> spot and not to run to the works committee. The
> atmosphere which we have here lets us do just
> that.

This view also stems from the rather free-and-easy
atmosphere in which things are not taken too strictly, so that there is less awareness of the different
positions and interest of employer and employee. The
free-and-easy atmosphere is also reinforced by the
very personal management style characteristic of the
company management. For the Managing Director, the
term 'personal' means that people should feel free
to express not only their positive but also their
negative side even though, as he (the Managing
Director) is fully aware, the highly individual and
personal management structures such a system produces can bring with it problems. For example, a
change in personnel can lead to a complete change of
emphasis:

> That happened for the first time in the 1970s
> when the senior partner died. The employees
> must learn to live with the problems not only
> of a change in management, but also the prob-
> lems related to changes of all these managers

and employees at Beck to whom they relate, as we all must. I myself am not always available and know that it is not necessarily quite the same if I am replaced for that moment by someone else, and that is the way it is with everyone in the company.

He also sees the problems which can arise in such a personal system, so dependent on individual relations if, for any reason, some of these links are missing. Inevitably when people leave, the networks they have built up tend to dissolve and the new people who join the company must forge their own links and create new networks. The high degree of motivation of the employee provides the energy which makes the system work.

A new freedom for creative development is afforded by the Beck concept itself which allows for innovation. It is expected that this freedom will be used with commitment and to innovate. A crucial effect of this has been on middle management who, partly for this reason, now have a very committed professional identity. Consequently, 41 percent of the female department heads find it extremely difficult to imagine combining a job and family - as compared with the sales assistants where the figure is only 12 percent; both the different way the two groups see themselves and their jobs and the objective difference in their workload play a part here. This means that the fact that Beck places such an emphasis on the family dimension of its employees' lives, women still have to make a decision: not between __job__ or family, but between career and family.

Although there is a highly positive side to the unusual recognition of the whole emotional dimension at Beck so that it is possible, for instance, for employees to get in touch with each other's feelings far more than is the case in other companies, something which corresponds to the way women tend to look at things in general, it also involves dangers and risks. 'Feminisation of the working world' demands high standards on the part of management if it is not to lead to economic exploitation. The atmosphere such an approach creates produces a willingness to work harder and more efficiently, and consequently to increase productivity, must not just benefit the company. A balance must be struck between what women give and what they receive. This certainly ought to apply to the wages paid, but equally it should also apply to flexibility in terms

The Beck Department Store: A Case Study

of time which then really does provide that little bit of freedom.

NOTES

1. See Tables 5.1 and 5.2 for a breakdown of respondents to the questionnaire and of those who participated in in-depth interviews.

The Beck Department Store: A  Case Study


Table 5.1: Structure of the Population Investigated
at the Beck Store:  the Questionnaire


| Structural features | number |
|---|---|
| All women questioned | 393 |
| Full-time | 165 |
| Part-time | 228 |
| Overall | 393 |
| With children | 184 |
| No children | 200 |
| Not specified | 9 |
| Overall | 393 |
| Married | 202 |
| Single | 106 |
| Divorced, separated, widowed | 85 |
| Overall | 393 |
| under 23 years | 40 |
| 23 - 27 years | 36 |
| 28 - 37 years | 64 |
| 38 - 50 years | 180 |
| over 50 years | 73 |
| Overall | 393 |
| Head of dept. | 15 |
| Departmental manageress | 27 |
| Saleswoman | 272 |
| Employees in the administration dept. and other depts. | 41 |
| Not specified | 38 |
| Overall | 393 |

The Beck Department Store: A Case Study


Table 5.2: Structure of the Population Investigated
at the Beck Store: In-depth Interviews

| Structural features | number |
|---|---|
| Female | 34 |
| Male | 9 |
| Overall | 43 |
| Full-time | 26 |
| Part-time | 17 |
| Overall | 43 |
| With children | 28 |
| No children | 15 |
| Overall | 43 |
| Age of the children | |
| less than 6 years | 8 |
| 6 - 14 years | 9 |
| 15 - 21 years | 13 |
| over 21 years | 9 |
| Overall | 39 |
| Married | 20 |
| Single | 10 |
| Divorced | 13 |
| Overall | 43 |
| under 28 years | 8 |
| 28 - 37 years | 9 |
| 38 - 50 years | 20 |
| over 50 years | 6 |
| Overall | 43 |
| Head of dept. | 14 |
| Departmental manageress | 3 |
| Saleswoman | 26 |
| Overall | 43 |

The Beck Department Store: A Case Study

## Table 5.3: Most Important Qualities for Sales Staff

Question: As an employee of a department store, selling is
your most important activity. For this reason we want to know

a) which qualities are,
in your opinion, most
needed in your job?
(Please don't check
more than three)

b) which of the above
mentioned qualities
come especially easy
to you?

| part-time % | full-time % | qualities | part-time % | full-time % |
|---|---|---|---|---|
| 75 | 73 | enjoy meeting people | 68 | 64 |
| 12 | 18 | fluency of speech | 10 | 12 |
| 4 | 6 | ability to improvise | 11 | 14 |
| 8 | 6 | to be restrained | 6 | 6 |
| 43 | 34 | to be able to listen to an-other's problems | 35 | 30 |
| 6 | 3 | be attractive; have the courage to dress in the latest fashions | 6 | 5 |
| 30 | 32 | be able to identify with the product | 20 | 20 |
| 63 | 75 | specialized knowledge (knowledge of the trade) | 30 | 33 |
| 4 | 3 | good physical condition | 3 | 3 |
| 46 | 43 | good nerves, ability to work under stress (for example, during rush hours) | 1 | 1 |
| 228 | 165 | total number of persons questioned | 228 | 165 |

In estimating the most important qualities for sales staff,
the following three answers predominated (see left side):

o enjoy meeting. people, dealing with customers, reacting to
other people

o specialized knowledge; indentifying with the product

o good nerves, ability to work under stress

The table shows that the first two categories are practically
identical with the respondent's own qualities, which shows a
high assessment of this occupational group.

It is also clear that other qualities for sales staff, such as
"good nerves", "ability to work under stress", "good physical
condition" are also recognized as problems.

160

Table 5.4: Advantages and Disadvantages of the Individual Worktime

Question: Where do you see the advantages and disadvantages of the individual worktime?

| | agree, strongly agree | | disagree, strongly disagree | |
|---|---|---|---|---|
| | part-time % | full-time % | part-time % | full-time % |
| fair record of hours actually worked | 95 | 91 | 1 | 2 |
| individual desires for changes on short-term notice can be taken into consideration | 75 | 68 | 6 | 5 |
| the increased workload during rush hours leads to greater job satisfaction | 64 | 54 | 13 | 14 |
| I have less nervous strain | 37 | 22 | 36 | 45 |
| the quality of work life has improved | 44 | 42 | 27 | 22 |
| not dependent on the favour of the superior in choosing time off | 47 | 41 | 30 | 33 |
| being free to choose the individual worktime gives a greater feeling of independence on the job | 40 | 39 | 28 | 22 |
| more consecutive days off | 59 | 54 | 18 | 20 |

Table 5.4 (cont'd):

| | agree, strongly agree | | disagree, strongly disagree | |
| --- | --- | --- | --- | --- |
| | part-time % | full-time % | part-time % | full-time % |
| electronic timekeeping is more precise | 32 | 39 | 51 | 48 |
| working in rush hours requires more concentration – thus more stress | 32 | 27 | 45 | 39 |
| always working with different colleagues affords less opportunity to make friends | 20 | 18 | 55 | 54 |
| it depresses me when I have any "minus" hours | 52 | 39 | 31 | 37 |
| lack of information | 18 | 16 | 57 | 57 |
| due to the large number of part-time employees, there is increased pressure to produce | 18 | 22 | 51 | 57 |
| have time off when I don't want it | 39 | 37 | 39 | 35 |
| the increased stress has a negative effect on my private and family life | 15 | 19 | 65 | 60 |
| total number of persons questioned | 228 | 165 | 228 | 165 |

All in all, the "Individual Work Hours" are considered a good thing. Even the full-time employees are of this opinion, although they can take less advantage of the system than part-time employees.

A real record of time worked and the fact that individual desires for changes on short-term notice can be taken into consideration are considered especially advantageous.

The employees view the many "minus" hours as a great disadvantage. "Minus" time accumulates when the salespersons work less than the agreed-upon number of hours, for example, during off-peak hours. They then usually must compensate for this by working more time during rush hours.

The Beck Department Store: A Case Study

Chart 5.1: Organisational Subdivision of Beck's Department Store

| | |
|---|---|
| Total number of employees | 810 |
| of these: in the parent store | 660 |
| of these: women | 561 |
| men | 99 |
| trainees (apprentices) | 95 |

COMPANY PARTNERS (9 men, 4 women)

COMPANY MANAGEMENT
3 Managing Directors (men)

SALES DEPARTMENTS
(18 female heads of dept., 4 male)

e.g. coats/suits, dresses, cosmetics, hosiery, curtains and linen etc., children's department

OTHER DEPARTMENTS

e.g. advertising, training, administration etc.

MAIN STORE (Munich)

| BRANCH Munich | BRANCH Munich | BRANCH New York |
|---|---|---|

All three branches are managed by women

# PART FOUR

# SOME PARTICIPANTS' PERCEPTION OF THE PROBLEM

Chapter 6

WORKING AT THE SUPERSTORE

Joy Kuhn

BEING A TILL OPERATOR (1)

Working as a till operator is a tiring job; people
think you are just sitting there not doing anything,
but you are. You are moving stock: in the years I
have been there, I must have moved the whole of the
stock of the Superstore through. As the customer
goes through the checkout the till operator has to
pick up each item with their left hand and put it in
the trolley - a big bag of potatoes can be very
heavy. People think 'That's a nice job, you are
just sitting there', but really you get very tired
because you are using a lot of muscles: you put
pressure on your back, in your feet, you really are
working every part of your body. I only worked
part-time, but even my shoulder, the one you used to
lift all the things into the trolley, sometimes
ached; I should imagine anyone who had done it all
day long must really ache across the back.
     As far as other people are concerned, it is
just a job with no skill attached to it, a job that
takes no effort, but what they forget is the stress
factor. All the time you are sitting on that till
you have to concentrate, customers are coming
through all the time and you cannot drop your concentration for a minute. It was very different in
the past. When I first started working 40 years
ago, the hours were much longer - the normal working
week for shop assistants was something like 48 hours
- but the pace was so much slower. Now, for nearly
all the three, or sometimes four hours, I was on the
till, I was going at full pitch.
     Years ago a customer would come in, you would
sell them whatever they wanted, you would have a
little chat and then perhaps you would get another
customer. You did not have a whole queue waiting

for you all the time; they came in for the whole
process; jobs have now been cut up into little
sections. It was so much nicer to go through the
whole process; serving the customer and taking the
money; it was so much more human. Nowadays you do
not look after your own stock. Years ago when I
worked at the Co-op, nothing was pre-packed; we had
to weigh and pack everything like sugar, dried
fruit, everything like that; so when there were no
customers, there you were weighing all this stuff
and packing it into bags ready for the customers
when they came in. Customers were people then, now
they come through the checkout like robots.

In those days you did not get anywhere near so
tired. I know that I am older now, but even the
youngsters at the Superstore get absolutely worn
out. People often say the youngsters do not work,
but they do, management expects every ounce they can
get out of them. Things are just so much faster
nowadays everyone has far more pressure put on them.
I know they have cut the hours down, but not to that
extent.

The management do not work out the kind of
stress that is involved in the job as it is nowadays. If it was something very important, say
someone's life was at stake, they would probably go
into all the stress factors, but because the effects
of this kind of stress are not so obvious, nobody is
bothered.


TRAINING AND COMMUNICATION

One of the real problems at the Superstore is the
lack of training; there is no real training. When
you start as a till operator you are put on a till
with one of the people who has been there sometime;
she stands behind you watching what you are doing,
and explaining how to work the till. As soon as the
Supervisor feels that you are ready, usually after a
few hours, you are put on a till of your own. But
as for understanding what the till does, or what
happens on the computer in the office, you are left
completely in the dark. Apparently before the store
was opened the staff were given two weeks training
and told exactly how everything works; there are
four of the original till operators left and they
thoroughly understand those tills. There is never
any bother with those four, so it shows you how
valuable that fortnight's training was. When I
started I was thrown in at the deep end: yes, I

could work the till, but I really did not know what
was happening, I only learnt as I went along. I
think everyone should have a proper period of training before they start on the tills, and the same
goes for everyone else, even the managers are not
properly trained - nobody is trained.
No-one is trained in how to deal with customers. Some of the youngsters, only because they
have not been properly trained, just have no idea
how to deal with customers: they glare at them, do
not say 'Good morning' or 'Good afternoon', or
'Hello' or 'Goodbye'. They have no idea how to
manage difficult customers. What they need are
training sessions in which people come up to them,
throw difficult questions at them and are generally
awkward, so that they can learn how to treat awkward
customers.
Just as the staff sometimes have problems dealing with customers because they have not been
properly trained, so too the managers, for the same
reason, often have problems dealing with their
staff. They do not seem to be able to discuss
things with their employees; a new rule is not
explained to the staff, it is just handed down. It
is never explained why this particular new rule has
been introduced. The way new regulations are introduced means somebody may have been doing a job a
certain way for years and suddenly it is changed,
but the person doing the job has not been told and
the next thing they know, they are being told off
for doing it wrong.
What would be a good idea would be to have
discussions every so often, in the canteen perhaps,
where the managers could get together with staff and
explain what is happening in the store and why. It
would also help the managers get to know their
staff, and the staff would get to know the managers.
As it is there are people there who have been working for months who do not know who the Store
Manager is. Some time ago, for instance, the
Manager went up to the tobacco kiosk and started
asking the youngster there all sorts of questions,
and she thought 'Well, this is funny, why is this
strange man asking me all these questions?' so she
said 'Would you mind telling me who you are?'. And
she'd been working there for months.
If only they were consulted, the staff might
improve the running of the store. It is the staff
who are actually doing the job, and if you are doing
the same job for months or years, surely you are
likely to know which is the most efficient way of

doing it? Of course not all the staff's ideas are
necessarily good ones, but would it not be better to
explain to people why they are not? I am sure one of
the reasons the store has such a high turnover of
labour is the attitude of the management; people
leave because they just cannot stand the way the
managers treat them. Some of the managers really
are like little Hitlers.

A good example of the sort of problem that
could be avoided, if there was more consultation
with the staff, are all the problems the till operators had when new checkouts were put in last year.
The first problem was that the new checkouts had
been built the wrong size. The office staff and the
security staff sat in them to try them out and they
thought they were fine, but they never thought of
asking any of the till operators to sit in them and
see how the whole checkout process worked. If they
had, the till operators would have at once known
that they were too small. But anyway, they put all
these new checkouts in and to reach the till you had
to sit side on, you could not get your knees under,
so we had to sit at an angle with our body all
twisted round. Even when they modified them, they
had put a ledge in so you still could not get your
knees underneath properly, and so they had to come
and saw off all the ledges.

Another problem is getting in and out of the
checkouts: they have put the opening on the wrong
side so that when you are getting in and out, you
have to say 'Excuse me' to the customer being served
at the next till, and manoeuvre yourself past them,
whereas if they had had the opening your side you
could have got out quite easily, because the
customer at your checkout is standing behind it
waiting to come through.

The chairs in the checkouts are also a problem.
The management moan 'We keep having to buy checkout
seats' but the thing is the chairs were not very
good quality in the first place. They need to be
good strong seats: management are under the
impression that you are just sitting there pressing
buttons. They forget you are lifting all the grocer-
ies and putting them in the trolley, so that you are
bound to put pressure on the back as you lift with
your left arm. You must also put pressure on the
back of the seat because you are sitting down.

Some of the till operators have been working at
the store for over five years, they are the ones who
should have been consulted, since they are the ones
who have to operate the system day in and day out

and know exactly what is involved.

PART-TIMERS

Something I have never understood at the Superstore is why part-timers are not allowed to go on the information desk at the checkout. There is nothing difficult involved, it is just a matter of authorising cheques, answering customers' queries or price queries from the till operators, fetching change and so on. The only part-timers who are allowed to go on the information desk are the school children who come in and work Saturdays and late nights Thursday and Friday. It is as if they did not trust the part-timers; and yet the shop could not exist without its part-time workers. If all the part-timers walked out they would have hardly any assistants. In the case of all those part-timers who work less than 17 hours a week, the store gets the extra benefit that they do not have to pay an insurance stamp for them.

WORK AND FAMILY COMMITMENTS

One way in which the Superstore could help employees who have children is by being a bit more flexible as far as working hours are concerned. Most of the women at the store, who have small children, save up all their holiday entitlement as long as possible, because if there are any problems at home, like a child being ill, they have to use their holiday time. So they try to hang on to those days until the end of the year just in case anything happens at home. The Superstore could be a bit more flexible about letting people make up time they have missed because they had to stay at home with a sick child or whatever. After all, there are not that many women at the Superstore who have young children, so it is only going to apply to a few of them. There should not be any problem if someone says 'I have got to take my child to the dentist tomorrow, she has got a bad tooth', or 'I have to rush off to hospital with a child'. I think they should automatically be paid the same and just make up the hours some other time.

SHORTER WORKING HOURS AND UNEMPLOYMENT

In Britain generally, they have made so many
people redundant, when what they should have done
was cut the working week so that more people could
be employed, surely that would be better than paying
out all the huge sums of money that are paid out in
unemployment benefit.


NOTES

1. Shortly after the research project at the
Superstore finished, Joy Kuhn retired and consequently this account is written in the past tense.

Chapter 7

LIVING WITH A FAMILY AND LIVING WITH A JOB

Margaret Riedel

When I think about my family, I often think: are we
really a family at all? It seems to me that we are
more like a commune where each individual member
goes about their own business, sharing out their
time among friends, family and all the other things
they want to do.

What does the word family mean to me? Well,
although I still think of the old cliche of a
father, mother and children: we haven't had a father
in our family for quite a long time now, sixteen
years in fact. For many years our family was me (the
mother), my older daughter and younger son - another
son lived with his father for six years - and now
our family consists of a mother and both sons.

Each one of us has their own affairs to attend
to. Mine means, depending on how the company needs
me, going to work for about five hours every day.
Including travelling time, I spend six to seven
hours out of the house every day, five days a week.
My older son is 20 and a painter's apprentice. My
younger son, who is 17, is at secondary school; he
has sports lessons in the afternoons, does a news-
paper round at the weekends and occasionally spends
time on a farm with friends.

Our living routine is quite well organised.
Each one of us takes a share of the household
chores, more or less unwillingly, and I am always
the one who has to nag others; I end up screaming at
them to get something done. That is my first big
problem: I always have to go a bit too far before
things go back to normal. This forces me to act a
role I don't really want, but which I end up
slipping into again and again. It is just the same
at work, which worries me and puts me in a terrible
situation with the people I work with.

It's good that I'm writing things down because

it helps me see the problem more clearly. If I try
to be more relaxed at home, then the bomb goes off
all the more at work and vice versa. At the same
time, I have always wanted to work together with
people like me, that is people who work quickly and
well without any problems. They say I'm a perfec-
tionist and very few people can stand that.

Although, when I think about it, I manage to
deal with the problem of combining work and family
pretty well because I knew ever since I was a child
- my parents had a small business - that I would go
to work and have a family. I never really thought
about it in detail. From the age of 26 to 31, I was
mainly a housewife, but I did also work from home
partly because we didn't have enough money. Later,
my husband went to university, and the marriage
broke up soon afterwards, and I went back to working
part-time in my parents' business in the mornings. I
spent the afternoons at home with my children and,
most of the time, they kept themselves busy so that
I also had enough time left for various voluntary
activities. When I was young, and during my marriage, I was involved in Sunday school and a gymnas-
tics club. Later, I joined the SDP (Social Democratic Party) and worked as a treasurer for the
committee, and I also had my work with the women's
section where I was a delegate and played a very
active part.

Actually, my problem is that my life is too
hectic. Pressure at work doesn't bother me, I can
deal with that. I enjoy my work, my boys, my household and my other activities. The only thing I'd
like is more help and support from the boys to make
life easier. That's what I miss. I often think, how
could I do all the things I do if I were married? I
have no answer to that question. My husband used to
be just as busy working shifts and with his voluntary activities. I used to accept all that and I
didn't find it difficult, we just followed what our
diary said... but at least I was independent of my
employer. How I would find that sort of life nowadays I have no idea, but I imagine that with all my
experience I'd manage as long as there was an understanding on both sides. Now I know I alone am
responsible, I'm the one in control and it's easier
to live with that way. The children themselves now
have their own rhythm and way of life, and we often
just say to one another, 'When will you be home?'

As far as my voluntary activities are concerned, in some groups I do the giving, but there
are also some where I am more of a taker. Whenever

people ask me about my life and I tell them all the
things I do, then even I think to myself: that's
quite a lot for one person to cope with. When people
ask me how I manage, I ask myself the same question:
how do I cope? Or even more, why do I cope? But
then the answer is easy: everything I do has to do
with people. I love people and want to be with other
people, and this gives me the energy to achieve what
I set out to do. When I'm tired and I think, 'Oh,
they can manage today without me,' then I tell
myself that if I don't go and others are thinking
the same, the person who has worked so hard to
organise whatever it is will feel let down and
frustrated, and all that work may go to waste. And
so I pull myself together and what's the result?
It's always beautiful!

Does my family help out? When I think about it,
yes. My daughter shares my political commitment and
so, too, does my elder son. My younger son likes to
live for himself, but then again at home he is the
one who always does his share without complaining,
and it is the others who always have to be reminded.
What about my partner? Until recently, when he
broke off the relationship, I had a boyfriend who
lived his own life, quite apart from my family, and
for whom I used to find time once a week or at the
weekend. I probably didn't give him enough time,
although it seemed he never really wanted me to get
too close to him. So I don't have any experience of
how it would work if I lived together with a partner. Although I think, and what I see around me
confirms me in this, is that it would be very difficult. I spend a lot of time with other single
parents who are willing to take time and commit
themselves to working for others, because it is we
who know best about loneliness and being alone.

Since I like my work and have time for my job,
my housework and my family, I don't have any problems I can't cope with. But it calls for a lot of
planning and I have to be disciplined about things.
The most important thing for me is that I don't have
to work full-time, so I can also involve myself in
various activities outside work and see some of my
ideas, even if only on a small scale, being worked
out in practice. If I needed more money so that I
had to overwork myself, I wouldn't have any energy
left for all the other things I want, and I would
certainly not enjoy the work I have to do to earn a
living. I would not have enthusiasm for anything and
would have a lot of problems which I don't have now.

Chapter 8

WORKING WITH WOMEN

Angela Fauth

We are a company employing more women than men, and
consequently well-acquainted with the tensions
which affect working women in trying to meet both
the obligations of their job and their family. We
take these problems seriously since this follows
from our belief that people should be treated as
entire people. This is reflected in our company
philosophy and also in the fact that our female
employees were the first people we consulted when
we wanted to introduce the IWT scheme. As far as
possible we have tried to fulfil the wishes our
staff expressed about their working hours. Perhaps
this differentiates us from other companies since we
really try to get to grips with the problems of our
female employees and do not merely make a show of
being interested. For us, family problems assume a
central position, and what we as an organisation can
do is to make work a little more family-orientated
for women. This was also the main reason why we co-
operated with this study. Of course, in 'normal'
companies the family in itself is not a topic for
discussion. The vast majority believe that the
family has nothing to do with the business at
working life. Generally, all our laws also reinforce
this attitude. For instance, laws on collective
bargaining and legislation covering working time are
completely outdated. The last time that legislation
on working time was reviewed was after the Second
World War, and the legislation no longer meets today's needs. In the reconstruction phase, after the
Second World War, there was a different awareness of
roles than there is today.
    Admittedly, this leaves us a certain latitude.
We have used this latitude, including all legislation on working time and collective bargaining, in
order to create something new, and are now seen as

something of a 'pioneer' in the retail trade. The only sad thing is that other companies tend to label us as eccentric or as mavericks, but we are not saying they have to adopt our IWT scheme - it would not be possible anyway since it is specially tailored to the needs of our company. But what our scheme demonstrates is that is is possible to take at least a step in the right direction, in spite of our antiquated and inflexible economic laws. For me this means extending the leeway we give our female employees and, together with this, an offer which enables saleswomen to combine both family and job.

Yet this only represents a first step. It is not an ideal solution, particularly as regards stress at the level of the individual. Of course we cannot, and do not want to, change the wider social conditions or to question the roles which the women internalise in the course of their socialisation. Our IWT scheme and our company philosophy only provide some slight assistance for women who want a paid job again after being at home looking after their families. For us, what this means is taking the person seriously, listening to the problems she is encountering on re-entering a completely different life and, possibly, helping her to find solutions. In very general terms it is all a question of a humane approach and, in particular, discovering what possibilities there are even given the basic employer/employee position. Naturally, this scope is restricted not only because of economic factors, but also because the company must treat all its employees fairly and justly.

One crucial point in personnel policy is to pay great attention to middle management. A little more humanity in everyday working life contributes greatly towards increasing production. The creation of this kind of people-centred approach is an important part of our training courses.

The IWT scheme was spcifically intended for women who had trained as saleswomen and who wanted to go back to their old job on a part-time basis after starting a family. Of course, it is also possible for women who have trained in other professions to come and work here, because if they are interested and like meeting people they can easily learn the job. We have a relatively low percentage of staff with many academic qualifications, and the level of education of our staff is similar to the average for the retail trade. However, our female employees probably have more chance of promotion than in other trades. It is easier to make a career here because it is personality rather than academic qualification which counts. This opportunity for promotion is especially important to women, and this is reflected by the high percentage of women we have in middle management, who started with us as trainees and are now either departmental manageresses or heads of department.

Another problem is the practical realities of combining a career and family. We have already begun offering our women middle managers the opportunity of working part-time. In this case what part-time means might be, for instance, that they work 160 hours per month instead of the normal 173 hours. To date only six departmental manageresses have taken advantage of this opportunity. Even such a small reduction in hours can be of great benefit to the individual since it means they have one or one and half more free days per month. We are considering the possibility of allowing two women to share one job, even at the level of head of department. The higher one goes, however, the more difficult is becomes. You first have to learn how to share the increased responsibility and the increased freedom of choice with a genuine team spirit.

Of course, it is difficult to make a real career as a part-timer. Even the female heads of department with children still work full-time, and naturally this causes enormous stress. We see this with all those with a family who have to work full-time. A general reduction in hours would be a help here.

What is missing in the IWT scheme , because it involves most of our women working two or three full days per week, is flexibility as regards looking after the children. Kindergartens and day nurseries have very rigid hours. Perhaps we ought to set up our own company kindergarten.

In quite general terms, regardless of family, making hours of work more flexible and being able to provide an individual work schedule is a crucial factor in terms of employees' motivation and, consequently, performance at work.

Chapter 9

PAID WORK, HOUSEWORK AND THE WORK ETHIC

Dennis Higgs

The study has awakened, in my mind, the need to be
more positive in examining the roles of female
labour within the Brighton Co-operative Society
(BCS). In common with all retailers, the Society
employs a very high proportion of part-time staff,
the majority of whom are women.
    The reasons why many women come into employment
on a part-time basis are of course many. I think
that one of the overriding needs is that women are
now expected to make a financial contribution to the
higher living standards more and more families are
now setting themselves. Such women tend to see their
work as having a secondary role in their normal day
to day life. This creates conflict for many women,
between responsibility to the family and their
employers. One result is that often female staff
fulfil very important supervisory roles, whilst not
wanting to formalise their supervisory status. It
was this fact which created an interest and willingness to participate in the Time Management research
project.
    The studies which Crehan conducted at
Peacehaven have given evidence of this kind of
contradiction in thought which seems to be
particularly apparent amongst those who, in the role
of a single-parent or single women, accept their
'lot' within the employment but have some hankering
for a more responsible position within the
organisation, and this in itself provides a cause
for interest and study.
    In the same context one has to examine the
reasons why the BCS, and indeed the whole of the
Retail Distribution Industry, employs such a large
proportion of female labour and so many part-timers.
There are many advantages from an employer's point
of view. First of all the part-timer gives a fair

degree of flexibility to the shop opening hours, which increasing competition now requires us to engage in. If you look at Peacehaven for example, the store is open for 57 hours a week, whilst full-time workers have a 39 hours contract. So there is obviously a fairly wide need for part-time labour.

It is interesting that when we were first re-cruiting in readiness for the opening of the Peacehaven Store, we drew from the immediate area a large number of people who came from a wider range of professions or jobs than that of retailing. Many came from banking, insurance, secretarial and clerical work, in addition to light assembly work. The applicants had been drawn to retailing because it was the only opportunity for employment, partic-ularly part-time in the area. There are other reasons than the simple financial ones, however, why women want jobs.

We are presently in a transitionary phase; the whole fabric of social life, including work and family, seems to be changing. In the retail sector change has come about with both female and male employees. Men predominate in managerial and super-visory roles and I am sure we don't give enough opportunity to women to engage in management super-vision. This may well be due to the fact that amongst males, much of their managerial development takes place in their early to mid twenties. This coincides with the period when women tend to leave to establish their families, and when they return to employment at around 30 to 35 years, family pressures limit them to part-time work of say, 16 to 20 hours a week. This makes any kind of career advancement difficult. When they move on to more extended hours, say 30 or upwards, however, then such opportunities for development are usually available. The conflict that then begins to develop is the role which the women see for themselves in the organisation. Along side this, there is always the attitude of the male Manager who has worked for the full period from 16 years of age onwards and who can't really identify with the problems of women. Thus women are not readily given opportunities, but nevertheless are relied very much upon for the specific skills they are able to develop: these are usually in the lesser areas of supervision, for example, section managers positions, provisions work, produce section manager, supervision of check-out operators etc. These in themselves have fairly limited skills which can be quickly learnt, but they do not necessarily give the opportunity for movement

into a more advanced management sphere and this is I
think where a great opportunity is being lost.
It is interesting to note that the Co-operative
College attempted to establish courses to give female staff greater opportunities in managerial
spheres and sought to identify the opportunities
for developing females as potential managers. A
formalised Management Development Course is now
available, and the most recent course was highly
successful.
In local terms, we have to examine what areas
of opportunity we would seek to establish and to
develop certain skills much more quickly than has
been the case in the past. There are many opportunities within the Society for following the formal
pattern of training; we have already appointed some
female managers from among those who have followed
the formal approach, but their management development took place during the 21 to 25 years age group.
I should mention that in BCS we have a couple of
particularly able and exceptional women managers. We
have now moved towards training potential female
butchers. This has come about as a result of the
early observations which were noted in this study.
We have had to do a fair amount of work in persuad-
ing senior managers that there was a positive role
that women could fulfil in this particular area,
remembering that women have a continuing and important place in the preparation of meat, and its
wrapping, packing, weighing and pricing in the
modern supermarket. It is not too far a step to
give them the opportunity of boning out meat and
developing the normal butchery skills that are
associated with the family butcher.
If the opportunity for greater involvement in
more senior positions within the organisation is to
be developed, then there has to be a clearer job
identity amongst women. A prime factor to be considered here is the attitude of the male within the
family. There is a considerable area of change that
has to take place in male understanding of the
conflict of the women's role outside her formal
work. This, I think, is at the centre of the problem
and there does not appear to be any easy solution to
this. One step which can be taken by the employer is
to positively develop a far greater awareness on the
part of all male staff of the need to give women
greater opportunities. This must begin in the
senior managerial positions and could fairly easily
be accomplished. What we have to bear in mind,
however, is that we have a relatively small number

of branches with possibly only one male manager supported by almost an exclusively female team. It is here that there is the possibility that managers may not readily accept the need for a changing role for women. Whilst women might present a challenge for managerial jobs within the small units, I don't see this as being a massive problem because retailing competition today means that women can easily be fitted into the smaller unit; i.e. community type of store; and can fulfil a very important role at a reasonably high level of trading in a job which identifies with the social environment in which they are both living and working. It is a fact also that the smaller units in themselves don't attract the most ambitious of males and, for this reason, we can develop within the small units the first class training for the ambitious amongst both sexes. Women can, therefore, easily take over the management of the small stores, accepting a salary scale which relates to the viability of the store and meeting the economic needs of those individuals with lighter earning requirements. To achieve this we may well have to adopt a more positive discrimination in favour of women, at least in the earlier stages, to establish new attitudes. This does demand a rethink on the part of senior managers and the Board of Directors in establishing what can be done in this sphere and would, of course, be time consuming. It wouldn't necessarily, in the short term, give direct repayment of the energy and finance invested in it, but possibly over a five to ten year period the Organisation could be all the better for adopting this approach.

The importance of achieving a change in attitudes of both male and female staff to the roles of women cannot be emphasised too greatly, together with the significant contribution which both will be able to make by extending their own visions beyond that of the very limited ones of the present time. These visions concentrate almost exclusively on shelf filling, check out operation and very limited skills within the total store operation, and thought must be given to this aspect of thinking within any training programme which might be drawn up.

If women are to take up more responsible roles at work, I guess they will have to be relieved of some of their domestic responsibilities. I am not too certain as to how far we, as employers, would be able to go in this setting. The question of creches; the problem of giving women such facilities as hairdressing and so on; these, I think, are very important and certainly would assist in increasing the overall status of the woman in the eyes of the employer. This, of course, could only be done at a cost, and given the large number of stores currently run by BCS, might not be an economic possibility. The provision of such facilities should certainly be given careful consideration, as should the possibility of having more residential, rather than the predominantly non-residential training programmes which most employers currently offer.

Any employer must be limited in the contribution they can make, and must look to Government and other social forces to shift male attitudes towards participation in childcare, housework and so on. Given that the majority of homes today have many labour-saving appliances, these duties should not be too difficult a task for most men given the right attitude. This does, of course, presume that there is something of a role reversal here, that the male will be spending far more time at home than has traditionally been the accepted position. Given the extension of the computer within our lives we can see the possibility of work being undertaken from home, as well as being undertaken on a part-time basis. This would allow many wives the opportunity of leaving their husbands in charge of the children.

I notice a change in young people's attitudes to the work ethic in that they do not see themselves as 'living to work' and many of them are rethinking the place paid work should have in their life in the present state of high unemployment; the time seems ripe for a reappraisal of our social attitudes. Men and women are realising more and more that work is a means to an end, to improving the quality of life, and are questioning the work ethic which has dominated our lives for the last century or so.

Of course, work is still an essential part of the framework within our lives. Each of us has to make some economic contribution to our existence, and thus it seems that whilst we have to work, then opportunities for women should be as great as those which apply for men. Possibly some of my thinking here is derived from the fact that I, myself, had to undertake a dual role of housekeeper and employee in order to sustain myself and a family of grown children. This inevitably made me face the problems of single parents. They are similar to those of married mothers, although the latter have the additional burden of supporting the husband in the male

Paid Work, Housework and the Work Ethic

role. In whatever family units individuals find
themselves, the needs of the children have to be
considered, and to a very large degree employment
has often to take second place. In my case, although I have always been very keen to develop my
career, when I had to meet the conflict of holding
the family together, then often work took a secondary role, whereas previously it would automatically
have come first.

Yet paid work still carries with it
considerable prestige. It is usually only paid
employment which carries with it some sort of social
recognition, and that's where prestige is established, to be seen fulfilling a specific role,
satisfying the needs of the community in the work
that you are undertaking. By contrast, the woman who
is undertaking the role of bearing and rearing
children is working very often in isolation. Too
often we assume that housekeeping is unskilled and
that basically anyone can do it. This is true to a
certain extent but efficiency is simply not measured
in the same way; the value is in social terms, i.e.
the rearing of an individual to be able to establish
a role within society.

It all depends, of course, where you place the
emphasis. Whilst as a parent one can look at one's
children and say 'I have created something which is
thoroughly worthwhile', society often does not
appreciate the role of the parent. I think this is
not peculiar to this country, but seems to be one of
the problems of being a parent: a universal dilemma
in which society finds itself. Bringing children
into the world is possibly one of the easiest of
activities, therefore it may well be that its true
value is not appreciated within society, and consequently all of the activities stemming from raising
and maintaining a family unit are minimised.

The work ethic seems to be disappearing, but
this change of attitude will not come overnight. It
is interesting that despite the considerable amount
of unemployment these days, to be unemployed seems
still to carry some sort of social stigma. Certainly I don't believe that the Government of today does
anything to lessen that. I don't think that anyone
should minimise the importance of work to the
individual because certainly it gives one a structure around which one can develop. It brings a
discipline which, in turn, creates a social contact.
If left to live in small nuclear units we wouldn't
necessarily develop from that point of view. Work
does fulfil an extremely important part of one's

total being, but I wonder if we have begun to reach the stage where practically any labour activity can be undertaken by some sort of robot or machine? If this is the case, then the work ethic may diminish rapidly.

As time goes on its significance will lessen further. I cannot honestly see how those who are living at the present time in very high unemployment areas - something like 12 to 17 percent - can even begin to identify with the work ethic at all. I know in my own case, as I am possibly approaching the end of my working life, my attitudes to work have changed considerably. I no longer consider it to be as overwhelmingly important as my father did at my age, and indeed his father.

Chapter 10

THE TRADE UNION & THE CONFLICT BETWEEN WORK & HOME

R.A.Hammond

The observations which I give below are purely my
own - they do not necessarily reflect the views of
my employer, the Union of Shop, Distributive and
Allied Workers. My views are expressed as a Trade
Unionist, as a senior Trade Union Official with
experience gained at local and national level within
the distributive industry and, in particular, the
retail trades. These comments are made in the knowledge of the tremendous changes which are currently
taking place in retail distribution, against a background of very high unemployment in the UK and
increasing competition by major employers to still
further reduce their labour costs.

As a Trade Union official my first concern is
to protect the interests of my members working within the industry. I cannot therefore, simply write
an academic essay on the social needs versus the
work needs of women. I write knowing that many
workers in retail distribution resent the increasing
number of part-time employees entering the industry.
They do so because they feel it could well undermine
their bargaining strength in protecting their existing rates of pay and conditions of employment. It
is not particularly easy to organise workers in
retailing for collective bargaining purposes. Therefore, as a Trade Unionist I have to always consider
very carefully the introduction of new work patterns
and the effect these may have on working conditions.

General unemployment and the continuing decline
of jobs in manufacturing, and the continual development of potentially labour-saving technology, provides a sombre background to the question of job
creation in the retail sector. Employment prospects
in retailing are of particular interest to women,
most of whose employment opportunities are concentrated on fewer industries than men's. The disper-

sion of shops throughout centres of population makes many jobs in retailing particularly accessible or convenient to employees. The location of shops near homes also means that retailing offers employment in areas such as inner cities and rural districts where other employment opportunities may be scarce.

Employers' interests in industrial relations can be correlated with the labour intensiveness of retailing. Efficiency largely depends on the effective utilisation and deployment of labour. Evidence suggests that the latest methods of trading are often more capital and less labour intensive. This puts even more pressure on marginal labour costs and has intensified efforts to make more effective use of employee hours. It has contributed to the increase in part-time employment.

The total number of individuals engaged in retailing (self- employed or employees) declined from 2.5 million in 1978 to approximately 2.2 million in 1982. There has been an estimated decline in the number of female full-time employees from 1.4 million in 1976 to 1.27 million in 1982. While total numbers of employed have increased there has been a decline in total manpower measured in terms of full-time equivalents from 2.34 million in 1961 to 2.13 million in 1971 to 1.88 million in 1976 and then to 1.6 million in 1982. This has been achieved by an increase in part-time employees who in 1982 represented an estimated 52 percent or 970,000 of all retailing employees. This is 9 percent more than in 1971. In 1982, 83 percent of part-timers were women. These figures (Census of Employment and Department of Employment Gazette) suggest that the availability of part-time employment has occurred almost solely because of economic rather than social factors. Employers have found that the costly new technologies demand the need to use installation effectively. Commercial pressure, particularly the search for increased productivity, has been responsible for the increase in investment. Commercial pressure has also contributed to focusing attention on the role of trading hours and wage costs.

Higher levels of unemployment among males and its effect on family incomes have, among other factors, increased the significance of women's employment and the income it can generate. The 1.5 million increase over the last twenty years of women in employment has been concentrated into four 'service' industries (60 percent of female labour is in education, medical services, distribution and miscellaneous services). The jobs created have, in general, been <u>low-paid</u>, lesser-skilled, mainly clerical and process work. In contrast with jobs lost in manufacturing, income from employment recently created contributes to, rather than maintains, average family incomes. Average full-time earnings in retailing in April 1982 amounted to 76 pounds per week, contrasting with an average household income of 176.67 pounds. As a Trade Unionist, I am concerned that an increase in part-time employment is eroding 'real' jobs.

It is estimated that 8.9 million female employees were part of the workforce in December 1983. By 1990 it is thought there will be an additional 460,000 women in the workforce, 330,000 more than the projected increase in males seeking work.

In theory, the retail trade offers a variety of work to both men and women in management, clerical, sales, merchandising and other jobs. In practice, the workforce is highly segmented. In 1981, about 85 percent of the sales staff were women, more than half of them part-time. By comparison, 65 percent of managers were men. The definition of managers is so wide and includes, for example, store and shop managers, departmental managers, and check out or provision managers. Although I cannot produce the evidence, my experience leads me to believe that less than 10 percent of female employees are in store managers' positions.

At a time when the number of females working in retailing has increased, the industry offers these women only low-paid, part-time jobs. The increased use of part-time staff who work sometimes as few as eight hours a week, presents all sorts of problems in trying to maintain, let alone improve the conditions of service of <u>all</u> workers in the industry. Part-timers working less than 15 hours per week are not covered by the protective provisions of the Employment Protection Act. Employers do not have to issue them with a Contract of Employment; they cannot go to an Industrial Tribunal for alleged unfair dismissal, are not covered by the Redundancy Payments Act and in fact have very little industrial employment protection. Their general conditions of service are also far worse than those offered to full-time employees. (The legal definition of a part-timer, is a person working less than 30 hours per week). Although there are exceptions, most part-timers do not qualify for sick pay or have any entitlement to a retirement pension. All in all, my experience shows that many part-timers are badly exploited.

There is some evidence that career prospects for a small minority of full-time women is improving. In 1974, 49 percent of university graduates entering the retail industry were women. By 1982 this figure had increased to 56 percent.

In 1982, nearly half of the retailing workforce worked for less than 30 hours per week and more than 80 percent were women. The prospects for employees working part-time are closely related to changes in the structure of retail trade and the resulting variable pattern of work. They are also affected by the extent to which retailers' requirements for part-time work match or mismatch with what people seek from a job.

RETAILERS' NEED FOR PART-TIME WORKERS

Three main reasons account for the high proportion of part-time working in retailing. First, part-timers are used to cover peak trading periods during the day, week or year. Secondly, some jobs do not last long enough to justify employment on a full-time basis. A third factor is that the costs associated with the implementation of various forms of employment legislation encourage the use of part-time workers in preference to full-time staff. For example, employer's National Insurance contribution has to be paid for those with weekly earnings above 34 pounds. The provision of legislation covering employment matters, such as The Equal Pay Act and the Sex Discrimination Act, offer differing forms of protection depending on hours worked and length of service.

While part-time staff may become costlier, the need for part-timers and their work conditions is becoming increasingly more complex. First of all there is the problem of how employment contracted conditions associated with the working week of 39 or 40 hours can be dovetailed with a trading week of up to 80 hours (including the possibility of widespread Sunday trading). Moreover, inequalities in the skills and experience of employees means that the allocation of hours requires thought not only about the number of hours, but how those hours are best used to take advantage of the variety of staff skills and expertise. There are of course also different skills required for different kinds of selling. For instance, personal contact with customers in specialist durable goods trading necessitates greater skills than to operate a till. Other variables which make for increased complexity in part-time employment are the shop location, length, duration and dispersion of opening hours; the variety in daily trading patterns linked with different locations, products and shop size.

WHY EMPLOYEES WANT PART-TIME WORK

Against the variable and increasingly complex need for part-time staff must be set the varied requirements of female employees, particularly those who are married. While in broad terms, women seek work for the same reasons as men, namely for income, companionship and often the desire to establish or maintain some degree of financial independence, there are also some significant differences. Women often seek work these days because of the reduced earnings or income contribution in times of recession, from other members of the family. Increased expenditure on such items as household durable goods or holidays which cannot be met from the current family budget puts pressure on women to generate additional income. For other women, financial independence makes them seek employment. This perception is related to the increasing rates of divorce and marriage separation. The availability and use of domestic electrical appliances which save time in carrying out a number of household tasks enable more women to take up paid employment. However, it is not easy for women to find the kind of job they want these days. First of all, because of the recession, there is now a lack of such jobs particularly in areas of high unemployment. Therefore women have jobs that can be quickly and easily reached from home and fit in with domestic needs. Most of the part-time jobs available now provide only sufficient income to contribute rather than maintain family budgets. The cost of travel to work, in time and money, may thus be too great to attract some women into lower-paid employment.

In general terms, a search for work within these constraints can lead to married women specifying job requirements in terms of: convenience to the home; hours of work and their starting and finishing time; work environment; pay and other contractual conditions of employment. Some of these requirements are more easily met by retailing than by other industries. The concentration of shops in surburban High Streets and in local neighbourhoods makes employment in shops an attractive proposition for women.

PART-TIME WORK: MISMATCHES IN DEMAND AND SUPPLY

In many cases, however, the specification of what women seek from work on the one hand and what retailers can offer may not always match. As a result, conflict or lost opportunities can occur. Prospects for part-time employment in the retail trade depend in part on how well such conflicts are anticipated and resolved and how keenly opportunities are grasped. The increased complexity of demand for part-time workers has resulted in attempts to allocate full and part-time staff work patterns around a set of core hours. This is reflected in a substantial increase in 1983 in part-time jobs offering eight to sixteen hours work per week, while there has been a considerable decline in jobs involving more hours per week. Moreover there has been a heightened need for some part-timers to equal the skills of full-timers in terms of merchandise and sales skills.

These recent changes in demand for part-time staff mean that nearly 25 percent of the total numbers involved in retailing work less than 16 hours a week; this includes 'Saturday only' staff. Accordingly, individual part-timers are likely to work fewer hours per week in the future than they might have done in the past.

HOURS

Extension of overall trading hours can increase the flexibility in the hours of work retailing can offer its employees. This can help married women dovetail work and domestic demands on their time. In so far as it makes access to part-time jobs easier, this could increase the number of people seeking part-time work.

On the other hand, pressures on operating costs encourage retail businesses to fit, as precisely as possible, staffing levels to variations in daily trading volume. The introduction of Electronic Point of Sales and the information it can provide could increase that precision. Greater precision in the pattern of staff requirement could reduce the choice in hours of work offered to part-time staff. The effect could be more acute where moves towards extension of trading hours into the evening and, perhaps Sunday, generate a demand for part-time staff at times when, for married women, the greater demand on their time is at home. In this case a mismatch between employee and business requirements could cause strains in female employees and their effectiveness in carrying out the job could decline.


PART-TIMERS' EXPECTATIONS

It is often claimed that the general employment expectation of a part-time employee is less than that of a full-time worker and that a part-timer regards income from the job as being secondary and is content to remain in that particular job. This view is becoming increasingly less valid and should not prevent the opportunity to promote part-time employment. Such a policy has already been adopted by some retail companies and others in business could ask why and how they might successfully follow this pattern.


CONCLUSION

The common perception of jobs available to part-time female workers in the retail trade, is that they compare less favourably with full time jobs. Generally they are routine, of lower status, and offer little prospect of career development above supervisory level. In the main, part-time workers lack the opportunity to ensure that they are as fully aware as full-time workers of various forms of employment protection legislation.
    The terms and conditions of employment of 1.2 million employees in the retail sector are currently covered by the two Retail Wages Councils. In earlier years, the Wages Councils were seen as a mechanism for establishing minimum wages and condi- tions of employment, and that in their absence wage levels and conditions would be socially and/or politically unacceptable. The emergence of Wages Councils as surrogates to voluntary collective bar- gaining shifted the emphasis from social and politi- cal standards to reasonable standards.
    The current Conservative Government has ques- tioned the role of the Wages Councils and made vague accusations that they are inflationary and that they have outlived their purpose. If in fact the Wages Councils were to be abolished, leaving workers in

retailing without any statutory legal pay minimums or minimum conditions, then this would have a very adverse affect on an industry where outside of the multiples, Trade Union organisation for collective bargaining is very difficult. I feel that part-timers would be particularly vulnerable to employers taking advantage of their weak bargaining position.

In examining the conflicting demands of work and home it is important that those who advocate greater freedom and flexibility of working hours for part-timers also consider the urgent need to ensure a maintenance of reasonable conditions of work. By and large, part-timers operate outside the legal protection from industrial legislation which, as I have already argued, covers particularly full-time employees. In addition one should not overlook the probable detrimental affects on the existing work-force by the increase in laissez-faire attitude to employment conditions.

Trade Unionists cannot ignore the continuing growth of part-time working, the problem of employment protection for part-time workers, the specific difficulties faced by women workers, particularly with the prospect in the UK of extended trading hours. Finally, Trade Unionists must fight against the abolition of the Wages Council system, because this would threaten minimum rates of pay and established conditions of employment. In an industry which, for economic and not social reasons, is already stretching working patterns to enable more women the opportunity for more part-time work, I contend that the Trade Union movement and society in general cannot and must not allow women to be further exploited in their labour conditions and/or for them to be manipulated into being a tool for the undermining of the conditions of the workforce as a whole.

REFERENCES

Census of Distribution, 1971
Department of Employment Gazettes (various)
Employment and Ministry of Labour Gazettes (various)
NEDO estimates
Retailing Enquiry, 1976

Chapter 11

LIVING WITH THE UNION

Sheila Morgan

I have had a very varied career: I have worked in
factories, on a farm, been a dental receptionist, a
caretaker, all sorts of jobs. For the last five
years I have driven a delivery van for a small mail
order company called Home Deliveries. I was married
when I was just over 16. My eldest son was born
when I was 17 and the younger one two years later.
Except for very short periods, I have always worked;
I have certainly had a lot of experience of juggling
work and family life. I joined the Union of Shop,
Distributive and Allied Workers (USDAW) when I
started working for Home Deliveries with whom USDAW
have a closed shop agreement. Ever since I became
active in the Union I have tried especially hard to
encourage other women to become active. How I have
tried to do this and the problems that are involved
is what this account is about.

When USDAW first sent me my membership card
they also sent me details of a correspondence course
called, 'Know your Union'. I had never been active
in a union before and I thought I would sign up for
the course. A few weeks later I got a phone call
from the firm's manager asking me if I was
interested in becoming a shop steward. If I was
interested it meant going away on a two week training course run by the TUC. Well, when the manager
rang I had not discussed it with my husband or
anything; I had never even been away, but I just
said yes. I went into work and we went through the
formalities of an election - nobody else wanted to
do the job. Then I came home, said I was going away
for a fortnight and we, my husband and I, went to
see his parents to ask them to help out with the
children. I remember my mother-in-law said to me,
'Well, alright Sheila, as long as it is just this
once.'

I went on the course and I thoroughly enjoyed
it. Before I went I had a lot of gut feeling about
what I thought was right, and what I thought was
wrong, but I knew nothing about the history of the
Trade Union movement at all. On that course I
learnt so much and I began to see things more clearly. I came back wanting to get more knowledge,
wanting to get involved, wanting to get more active.
The first thing I did, when I came back, was to
phone up the local organiser and ask when the next
Branch meeting was. The organiser confessed that
the Branch had not met for nearly three years but
said, 'If you would like to book a room we'll call
a Branch meeting.' So I did. The first meeting we
held was in the November, and this is the time of
year when delegates are elected to go to the annual
conference. Since I was the one who had had the
initiative to get the Branch going again the
organiser proposed that I should be the delegate,
and this was agreed. Also at that meeting I was
elected chairperson. I came home really excited,
but I kept thinking about my mother-in-law saying,
'Well, it's alright as long as it is only just this
once.' I thought, 'How am I going to tell her?'
Gradually the family and I worked out a pretty
good system and nowadays things run reasonably
smoothly. As we see it, we are all part of one
household and we all have specific tasks and roles.
When I am out at work I do not expect to come home
and to have to do all the housework, all the cooking
and so on, and I do not. As I have got more and
more involved in my Union my husband and children
have taken on more and more responsibility for the
home. Of course, my children are older now so that
makes it easier. My family understand how important
my Union work is to me and they have been very
supportive.
In 1981 and 1982 I was nominated by my Branch
to go to the Union's summer school at Ruskin
College. There are a range of topics you can choose
from and in 1982 I decided to do the course on new
technology, because I work for a mail order company
which is making more and more use of new technology.
When I came back from this course I was able to talk
to the bosses about the new machines in a way that
nobody else could. Before I went they would talk
about software and hardware and I did not know what
on earth they were talking about; but when I came
back and they said they had decided to get VDUs I
knew exactly what they meant. Bosses do that to
you. They talk in terms they think you cannot

understand so that you have to stop them and say, 'Excuse me, would you mind explaining what that is.' It's a bit of a put-down for a steward because the boss knows what he is talking about and by using abbreviations you do not understand, he is showing you how superior he is. I quite startled them when I came back from Ruskin and I thought, 'Well that was very useful.'

As well as the Ruskin courses I did various correspondence courses through the TUC. When the elections came up in 1982 I was nominated for the Divisional Council, The Labour Party Conference, the Conference of Labour Women, and USDAW's substitute parliamentary panel. I thought to myself, 'That's four things, I'm bound to get one.' I got all four. Then a job as organizer came up in Southern Division in 1983 and I applied for it as it seemed this was the best way I could use all the various things I was learning. For the first time in my life I had found something I really wanted to do. Before I went for the interview it was said to me, 'Of course we're a bit loathe to put a woman in Southern Division because we had a nasty experience with a woman.' I did not get the job. I am not saying I did not get the job because I was a woman, after all it was my first attempt.

As far as my Branch is concerned I make a special effort to encourage women to come to meetings. One thing that puts a lot of women off coming to meetings is the fact that so often they are held in pubs. Personally it does not worry me, but there are a lot of women who never go in pubs and would not dream of walking through a pub to a room at the back all on their own. Since that first meeting I initiated, our Branch has grown enormously; now we get something like 40 people turning up to the Branch meetings. To get people to be active in the Union it's very important that when somebody shows enthusiasm it is nurtured and they are given support. At the moment I have got a deputy steward and she is fairly new; she has got the makings of a good steward but she is still worried about attending meetings on her own, so I make sure I am at every meeting with her. What I do is split the points we are going to raise in half, we discuss it beforehand and I say, 'I'll raise these points and you raise those.' I do not give her all the easy ones and take the difficult ones myself, I give her exactly half. If there are going to be a couple of things that are going to be no trouble, she gets one and I get one, and the same with difficult points.

It is only by tackling difficult points that she is
going to learn and develop the necessary confidence;
it is no good me always doing the ones that require
a bit of thought.

One thing that we do in our Branch which is
very important is not only to notify all work
places where and when the Branch meetings will be
held, but also I always take any new member's name
and address and anybody who has ever attended a
Branch meeting gets an individual card inviting them
to the next one, so that wherever there is interest
and a potential for activity I try and keep it going
by making it a bit more personal. It makes us, I
think, a bit less formal and bit more like a big
family. Things have certainly changed as far as our
workplace meetings are concerned; it used to be that
you could not keep members in the canteen once it
was time to clock off - meetings would start at five
to three and be over by ten past. But since I have
taken over I can keep them in that depot as long as
is necessary; I have kept them in that canteen until
quarter to five before now when there has been a lot
of business to get through.

It is interesting that although women are still
in a minority in my depot, it seems to be the women
who are most active in the Union. Sometimes women
who want to be active in the Union can have a bit of
a problem with their families and particularly their
husbands. When this happens, if it can help, I will
go and have a chat with the husband and try and
reassure him. But basically what I say to the woman
is:

> It's entirely up to you. You know your hus-
> band; I can say a word for you and I can give
> you a shoulder to cry on if you need it, but if
> you think getting involved with the Union might
> wreck your marriage then you have to make the
> decision whether if that is all it takes to
> wreck the marriage then perhaps the marriage
> was not worth it in the first place; or whether
> for you, becoming active in the Union is not
> worth the risk to your marriage.

As I see it, those are the only alternatives, because once you get started into the Trade Union
movement, really into it, it demands a commitment
you cannot go back on.

Since becoming active in the Union I have become far more confident, and because of this I have
been able to help and encourage loads of people.

For instance I know how to deal with the Social
Security; years ago when I personally needed help I
did not have the confidence or the knowledge, but
now I have been able to get people into Council
accommodation, because of the confidence I have
found. For some people increased confidence is the
main thing they get out of being active in the Union
and if only ten people have got a bit more
confidence to help somebody then everything I have
done has been worthwhile; everything I have been
through has been worthwhile because those ten people
are going to meet another ten people, and they will
meet yet another ten people, and that is how it goes
on.

Although I have never seen myself as a hardline
feminist, I find myself fighting a lot for women's
rights and general equality for women; being a woman
you tend to find yourself expected to be the spokes-
person on women's issues. For example, at a conference a couple of months ago somebody was invited
as a speaker to talk about Trade Unions and poli-
tics, and then I had to give the women's position,
but really this should not have been necessary; the
main speaker should have had sufficient knowledge
and have been sensitive enough to the implications
for women so that a specifically female response
would have been unnecessary. I could have handled
the main topic as well, if not better than him, but
I was not given the opportunity; the attitude tends
to be, 'We had better put in something about women,
Sheila can do that', but I do not know things just
about women. It is this sort of patronising attitude
towards women that we have got to change as women
within the Union. We are pressurised and kept down
by the top; they do not think we are capable. There
might be one or two women who get through the net,
but as a group we are not even thought of; they just
do not see us. We are seen in the branches, and
women are active in lots of branches not just mine,
but that is where it stops. Activity among women
stops at the level of the Branch in USDAW. When I
see all these men at conferences, sometimes I wonder if they are all kept in a cupboard somewhere,
and then brought out at conferences.

Although I will have a laugh and a joke with
the men, I have got a lot more sensitive than I was
a few years ago about things like sexist jokes.
Little things can mean a lot; I am very sensitive
for instance to women being called by their christian name while men are given a title. I feel we
should <u>all</u> be called by our christian names, or <u>all</u>

be given a title. Then again last night I was at a
meeting and the chairman said, 'Well, I'm past
retirement age, it's time I handed my job over.
There are young men who could fill the job.' Now
that gets to me, because in his mind there is no
place for a woman to fill the job. Without going
overboard and demanding that we talk about person-
hole covers, I do see a term like chairperson or
chair as being an equalising word that offers the
opportunity to a man or a woman. Similarly, when a
list of candidates is given I would like to see just
the initial and the surname, no Mr, Mrs or Miss, so
that the sex of a person is not an issue.

At our depot we have had a bit of trouble with
sexism from the men. They put a nude calender in
the canteen and all the remarks were getting a bit
much, so we asked them to remove it and when they
refused we put a men's calender up. They soon took
the women's calender down. In general, however, the
attitude of the men to the women in the depot has
improved; and I think what has helped is the fact
that the women stewards have looked after them at
work; we have negotiated for them and I was the
first steward in the history of the company to get
someone his job back after he had been dismissed.
Also I won the first tribunal case, so they know I
know the ropes.

One problem for any new member when they join
the Union can be all the formal jargon, proposi-
tions, motions, composite motions, amendment,
addendum and all the rest; all the people who come
to our Branch meetings are given a sheet which
explains all these terms. Our Branch meetings are
also deliberately kept very informal. We encourage
everyone to take part in discussions, and everything
is fully discussed, but at the same time we make
sure we get through all the necessary business. The
chairperson will say, 'Well, I think we ought to be
getting on to the next business so we will wind up
the discussion' and it all happens so smoothly that
people do not realise that they have gone completely
through an itemised agenda.

We also invite speakers to meetings; for instance if there is some dispute going on in the area
we will invite a speaker to come and put their side
of the story to us. We try to get a wide range of
speakers, we will have discussions on the Third
World, on South Africa; we try and get a wider look
at the world, because we have just finished work
and we want to hear something other than work. It
is important, however, that the speaker does not

stand there speaking for an hour and a half; the speakers we have generally just start off with a few points and the rest of the time is given over to questions from the audience. This way everyone takes an active part, and it is this plus the informality that makes our Branch meetings popular I think.

One reason that stops women from getting beyond Branch level in USDAW is all of the travelling and having to spend time away from home. Another reason is that conferences are generally held on a Sunday and a lot of women have to cook the Sunday dinner. For a lot of families Sunday may be the one day in the week when all the family get together and the Sunday dinner is very important. The way conferences are organised just does not encourage women to come to them; there are no creche facilities, often there is an overnight stay involved where people have to travel up Saturday night for a conference on the Sunday, this is difficult for many women to organise. Then the conference meetings tend to be very formal, men seem to have to be so formal about everything - the secretary is popping up and down like a Jack-in-the-box when somebody gets up to speak. They do not see how hilarious it is when you are sitting there and all you see is this secretary jumping up and down. You should be able to control a meeting without all these high-faluting titles, and all this ritual puts the women off.

It is especially difficult for women at conferences which involve an overnight stay. The men all immediately get together because the one thing they have got in common is the bar. Well, most women have been brought up not to stand at the bar, but to sit at a table and let the man bring the drinks, so they are isolated for a start, but it is just the initial step that is difficult. Once women have formed a group I think they make a much stronger, more closely-knit group than any males will.

A lot of these problems are difficult to do anything about, but one way is to build women's confidence from the Branch itself so that when they are delegated to go to a conference they are prepared. You say to them, 'You might find the first one or two conferences a bit difficult until you get to know some of the people there.' I have always made a point of introducing my delegates and visitors to all the people I know. I do not think a lot of Branch secretaries do that.

It is the first Union meeting you go to that
either encourages you or puts you off. I always get
to the room before the meeting starts and I can
generally pick out who the new people are because
I've got to know all the others. Well the first
thing I do before the meeting starts is go and
introduce myself, who I am, take them along to the
chairperson, introduce them to the chairperson, then
we get their name before the meeting starts. When
the meeting starts the first thing we do is welcome
the new members and we say, 'Brother or sister
from...', what workplace they're from and then,
when we've mentioned all those we think are the new
members, we ask if there are any new members so
that somebody who we've missed is not sitting in the
middle of the room thinking, 'I haven't been welcomed, what's wrong with me?' That's the first
thing we do. Then when people speak they always
give their name and where they're from so that other
people can make a mental note of it. The first
meeting you hardly ever remember any names anyway,
it is a bit of a formality. Why we do it is not as a
formality but so we get used to each other's names
and learn them. Then we give them the 'bumph' about
the order of things at the start of the meeting and
at the end of the meeting we generally have a chat
with the new members about their workplace, if it's
a new place particularly. Generally speaking the
first time they come along to the meeting it's
because they've got a problem.

We always have a slot at the end of the meeting
where we leave enough time for the members to have a
word with the organiser. Now he generally comes
along to the meetings unless he's got something else
on, but we've got this slot. So they have a word
with the organiser so they also get to know who the
full-time official is. That surprisingly generates
a lot of interest because the Union isn't so out of
touch then, it's come in closer. We ask them if
they've got any problems about attending Branch
meetings; if they've got transport, if they need a
lift if public transport is difficult: we encourage
those members with transport to give other members a
lift. From their first meeting we make it clear to
any new member that any Branch member who needs
travelling expenses to come to Branch meetings can
claim them. Also the Branch always has some refresh-
ments, some members can come straight to the Branch
meeting from work and have a sandwich and a drink.

Why have I become active in the Union? Perhaps
it was because I felt so defenceless and I could see

the struggles that had gone on; my own particular struggle was nothing compared to what has gone on and what people do go through. It made me want to help them because I am only a small cog. There's thousands around who are all doing their bit. When it all boils down to it I've never wanted advancement, I've taken positions because I've seen it as being of use, as a tool. I've seen Divisional Council help me with the Branch and I've been able to help more people as a Divisional Councillor. I've seen taking on the position of Secretary of the Branch and the knowledge I have acquired from it as helping more people. If I saw somebody coming up who would make a better job of it than I, then I would gladly go because the reason they are coming up is because I've encouraged them. I wouldn't hold on to the job of Branch Secretary and I wouldn't put myself up for re-election if I thought somebody was there ready to take over. You can lose people, there is a time when people are ripe to take on a job and if you stop them at that point you could lose them; I don't want to lose anybody to the movement because I think there's another role I can play further along. But I wouldn't push anybody or assist anybody until they'd learnt enough to be equal about the sexes; until they'd got that little bit extra encouragement. At the same time you mustn't let women go off into a corner on their own. Okay, sit them with another woman but sit them amongst men; don't segregate them; don't let them think they need to form groups of their own as a power base, because women shouldn't have to form a group as a power base. Women and men mix equally in my Branch and that's how it's going to stay. I don't want a women's section of my Branch because in our Branch meetings women are treated equally by me and they are given equality of opportunity. Sometimes it means spending more of the Branch funds on women to give them the equality of opportunity but that's what they get: equality of opportunity. When women are given equality of opportunity you won't need certain places reserved for women because everybody will be aware of the problems of women.

**PART FIVE**

**CONCLUSION**

Chapter 12

HOW THE OTHER HALF WORKS

Kate Crehan

In this study what we have tried to do is to provide
some in-depth accounts of the reality of the lives
of a number of different groups of women, all of
whom work in the retail trade, and all of whom,
although in different ways, are faced with the daily
struggle of fitting together their obligations as
employees with their obligations to their families.
Each of these two spheres, that of formal employment
and that of the domestic world of the family, have
their own rather different hierarchy of values, and
the contradictions between these are again something
that confront women not in some intellectual
abstract sense, but in the concrete choices they are
continually forced to make. Should they work, or
ought they to stay at home? Should they accept
promotion, or will this mean their family will
suffer? Their teenage daughter is going through a
difficult patch, are they justified in taking time
off work?
    Our studies focused almost exclusively on women
because although the problems of combining a job and
family life also affect men to some extent, it is on
women that society places the primary responsibility
for the welfare of the family; men discharge their
obligations to their family, at least according to
the ideology, by going out and earning the
necessary money. While some shifts may be taking
place in the nature of gender roles, the present
reality, and most likely that of the foreseeable
future, is that balancing family and job is overwhelmingly a problem for women rather than men, and
above all for mothers with school age and younger
children.
    Very importantly it is not just that women have
obligations to their families, it is also their
family life that gives the central meaning to their

existence in a way that it does not to men. They want to enjoy their children and give them time, but at the same time they want, and need, to participate in the world of social production and paid employment. This basic female dilemma of how to combine paid employment and family life was found by our researchers to be basically the same in Britain and West Germany.

Also common to both countries is the generally disadvantageous position of women within the labour force as a whole. With the exception of that small minority who can aspire to middle-class professional careers, both British and German women are confronted by a highly gender-specific job market that discriminates against them in terms of the range of jobs open to them, the wages they receive and opportunities for promotion. While women are entering the labour force in ever increasing numbers, a good part of this increase, in both Britain and West Germany, takes the form of part-time work. Whatever the reservations of trade unionists - despite the very considerable differences between the trade union movement in Britain and in West Germany, trade unionists in both countries seem to share a very similar attitude to part-time workers - the growth in part-time working seems inevitable. One of the most important conclusions of both the British and German studies was that if women are to receive a fairer deal in terms of their double burden, then it is crucial that part-time workers stop being seen as somehow not 'proper workers' with no real commitment to their job, with neither the right to any kind of opportunities for promotion, nor the full protection afforded to full-time workers. If we stop for a moment taking as the norm the male worker, and look at the world of employment from the point of view of women for a change, the implication for both Britain and Germany is clear: the whole pattern of employment needs to be fundamentally rethought. Being a conscientious parent and being a conscientious worker should not be competing options that individuals must choose between, it ought to be possible to be both. In order for this to happen there needs to be a much greater degree of flexibility as regards patterns of work and the perjorative attitude to part-time work and part-time workers must change.

In fact, of course, a whole range of flexible work systems are already in existence and new variants are being added all the time. By and large all these developments are viewed with grave

suspicion by German and British trade unionists
alike, and undoubtedly it is true that such schemes
tend to be introduced by employers not with the
altruistic aim of improving the quality of life of
their employees, but in order to suit their own
needs for a more flexible workforce. What the Beck
example shows is that it is possible to devise
schemes which serve the interest of both employer
and employees. If the trade union movement is to
genuinely represent the interest of large numbers of
its women members, ought it not to be taking a more
constructive attitude towards such schemes and
looking at how flexibility can be introduced in
such a way that it benefits workers and not just
management? Similarly, in West Germany, the trade
unions oppose the expansion of part-time work and
instead advocate a reduction in the working week, as
if these two alternatives were necessarily mutually
exclusive options. Rather than regarding the increasing number of female part-timers as a danger
signal to the bargaining position of unions, would
it not be better all round if trade unions began to
give priority to the plight of many female part-time
workers who have to work under below-standard
conditions just because they operate outside legal
protection? Surely, it ought to be possible for
trade unions to take on board the problems facing
female part-timers and fight for their working
conditions also to be covered by legal protection?

One interesting difference between Britain and
West Germany is the quite different attitude of the
state to the family. In West Germany the family is
seen as an important and specific area of concern
for any Government, and this is reflected in the
fact that there is a special ministry for 'Youth,
Family and Health'. The whole topic of the
integration of the sphere of formal employment with
that of the family is, therefore, highly politi-
cised. In Britain, although the issues raised cannot
be divorced from political questions, the prevailing
ideology is that the state has no business inter-
fering in family life. This difference may go some
way to explaining why the Beck employees seem to
have had such a much more explicit sense of belonging to a specifically female culture than did the
women at the Superstore or Roberts Bros. In line
with this stress on the notion of a specifically
female culture, the values of which derive from
family life and are often in conflict with those of
the male world of employment with its strictly
economic rationale, the German study argues power-

fully that the values of this culture, for so long suppressed and subordinated, need to be brought into the male dominated world of employment, if women are to achieve anything more than the status of second-class men within this world.

Something that was shared by all the women we talked to in both countries, however, was their general assumption that the problems they face in combining a job with family life are their own personal problems and it is up to them to find their own solutions. In fact, of course, the basic constraints within which individual women negotiate their own particular solutions are laid down by such factors as childcare facilities, the kinds of jobs available to women and so on, and it is to factors such as these that we must look for an explanation of the differences and similarities between the broad patterns of the shape of women's lives in the two countries. Our studies were too small-scale to say much about this macro-level, our concern was rather to illuminate how such macro-level structures are refracted through the lives of individuals and transformed into a lived reality.

As we stressed at the outset of this study, our aim has been to raise questions rather than provide solutions. All the contributors, researchers and participants alike, have provided their own slant to the fundamental questions we were concerned with, but there is a general and important consensus that the issue of how the worlds of family and paid employment fit together, is a crucial question for governments, trade unionists, industry and individual employees themselves. The decision makers of our society are overwhelmingly male, and because this issue primarily affects women it tends all too often to be ignored. But whether we like it or not, we live at a time when, for a whole host of reasons, there is a profound restructuring taking place in long established patterns of work. This process includes both radical changes in the nature of work, and changing perceptions as to the place work should occupy in people's lives. Determining the final form of this restructuring is a struggle between a wide range of competing interests, and let us end this study with a plea that the interest of women, and families generally, should be an important factor in reshaping patterns of work and that the trade union movement and the political parties (industry cannot but be expected to represent its own interest here), in both Britain and West Germany, seriously address themselves to these issues and begin genuinely to represent the interests of women, and indeed of all those who would like to see a more balanced and humane society.

BIBLIOGRAPHY

BRITISH PUBLICATIONS

Official Publications and Records

AAS (Annual Abstract of Statistics). HMSO, London, 1984.
ARGB (Annual Report for Gt. Britain Part I). HMSO, London, 1981.
BJFG (Bundesminister fur Jugend, Familie und Gesundheit). Familie und Arbeitswelt, Verlag W. Kohlhammer, Stuggart, 1984.
DES (Department of Education and Science). Statistical Bulletin, 5/84, HMSO, London, 1984.
DOE (Department of Employment). Employment Gazette, Vol 92, No. 4, HMSO, London, 1984.
------------------------------Manpower Paper No. 9, Women and Work a Statistical Survey, HMSO, London, 1979.
GHS (General Household Survey). HMSO, London, 1981.
Hunt, A. Management Attitudes and Practices Toward Women at Work, HMSO, London, 1975.
Martin, Jean and Roberts, Ceridwen. Women and Employment a Lifetime Perspective, Department of Employment, Office of Population Censuses and Surveys, HMSO, London, 1984.
The Observer, p.5, 26. Aug. 1984.
OPCS Monitor. Divorces 1982, Government Statistical Service, 1983.
--------------Ward and Civil Parish Monitor: East Sussex, CEN 81 WCP 14, Government Statistical Service, 1984.
Ramprakash, Deo. Social Trends No. 14, HMSO, London, 1984.
WS (Wirtschaft und Statistik). Ergebnisse des Mikrozensus, 1982, 1984.

# Bibliography

## Other References

Campbell, Beatrix (1984). Wigan Pier Revisited,
  Virago Press Limited, London.
Caplow, Theodore (1954). The Sociology of Work, of
  Minnesota Press, Minneapolis.
Cole, G.D.H. (1945). A Century of Co-operation,
  Co-operative Union, Manchester.
Co-operative Retail Services Ltd, The Circle of Co-
  operation, Manchester, undated.
Cunnison, Sheila (1983). 'Participation in Local
  Union Organisation, School Meals Staff: A Case
  Study', in Eva Gamarnikow et al (eds.) Gender,
  Class and Work, Heinemann, London.
Davies, Ross (1975). Women and Work, Hutchinson
  & Co Ltd, London.
Edgell, Stephen (1980). Middle Class Couples,
  Allen & Unwin, London.
Elias, Peter and Main, Brian (1982). Women's
  Working Lives, Institute of Employment
  Research, University of Warwick.
Fleuter, Douglas L. (1975). The Workweek
  Revolution, Addison-Wesley Publishing Company
  in the Philippines.
Galenson, Marjorie (1973). Women and Work in Inter-
  national Comparison, Cornell University, New
  York State.
Garmanikow, Eva et al (eds.) (1983). Gender, Class
  and Work, Heinemann, London.
Gutek, Barbara A., Nakamura, Charles, Y., Nieva,
  Veronika, F. (1981). 'The interdependence of
  work and family roles' in Journal of Occupa-
  tional Behaviour, Vol. 2.
Hakim, C. 'Job Segregation trends in the 1970s',
  Employment Gazette, December, 1981.
Hunt, Judith. 'Organising Women Workers' in Studies
  for Trade Unionists, Vol.1, No.3, WEA, 1979.
Hunt, Pauline (1980). Gender and Class Conscious-
  ness, Macmillan Press Ltd, London.
Jeffries, James B. (1954). Retail Trading in
  Britain 1850-1950, Cambridge University Press.
Kamerman, Sheila (1980). 'Managing Work and Family
  Life: A Comparative Policy Overview' in Peter
  Moss and Nickie Fonda Work and the Family,
  Temple Smith, London.
Land, H. (1978). 'Sex-role stereotyping in the
  social security and income tax systems' in
  Chetwynd T. and Hornett, O. (eds.), The Sex
  Role System, Routledge & Kegan Paul, London.
McIlwaine, Gillian, M. et al. 'The Scottish Peri-
  natal Mortality Survey' in British Medical

# Bibliography

Journal, Vol. 1979, p. 1103.
Moss, Peter and Fonda, Nickie (1980). Work and the
    Family, Temple Smith, London.
Oakley, Ann (1982). Subject Women, Fontana.
Raphael, Edna, E. (1974). 'Working women and their
    membership in labour unions' in Monthly Labour
    Review, Vol. 97, No. 5.
Rapoport, Rhona and Robert N. (1976). Dual-Career
    Families Re-examined, Martin Robertson.
---------(1978) Working Couples, Routledge & Kegan
    Paul, London.
---------(1980) 'The Impact of Work on the Family'
    in Peter Moss and Nickie Fonda Work and the
    Family, Temple Smith, London.
Rimmer, Lesley and Popay, Jennie (1982). Employment
    Trends and the Family, Occasional Paper No.
    10, Study Commission on the Family.
Sengenberger, Werner (1984). 'Developments and
    Trends in Economic and Labor Market Policy in
    the USA, Great Britain and the Federal Republic
    of Germany', mimeographed, unpublished paper.
Shankland, Graeme (1980). Our Secret Economy, Anglo-
    German Foundation, London.
TUC (1983). Working Women, TUC.
Werjcmen, Judy (1983). Women in Control, The
    Open University Press, Milton Keynes.
Women's Studies Group (1976). Women under Attack,
    Special report by Counter Information Services,
    Anti-Report, No. 15.


GERMAN PUBLICATIONS


Official Publications and Records

BMA (Bundesminister fur Arbeit und Sozialordnung,
    Hg.) Tatsachen, Entwicklungen, Erwartungen
    und Verteilung der Arbeitszeit, Forschungs-
    bericht Nr. 44, Bonn 1981.
BMJFG (Bundesminister fur Jugend, Familie und
    Gesundheit). Familie und Arbeitswelt. Gut-
    achten des wissenschaftlichen Beirats fur
    Familienfragen beim BMJFG, Bd.143 der
    Schriftenreihe des BMJFG, Bonn 1984.
------(Hg.) Frauen in der Bundesrepublik, Bonn 1984.
Deutscher Bundestag (Hg.) Die Lage der Familien in
    der Bundesrepublik Deutschland - Dritter
    Familienbericht,

Bibliography

Other References

Arzberger, Klaus (1982). Ausdifferenzierung des Staates und Differenzierungsprozesse im politischen System heute. In: Hondrich, Karl Otto (Hg.): Soziale Differenzierung, Langzeitanalysen zum Wandel von Politik, Arbeit und Familie, Frankfurt/New York.

Backer, G (1981). Teilzeitarbeit und Individuelle Arbeitszeitflexibilisierung - Festschreibung der Benachteiligung von Frauen in Beruf und Familie. In: WSI-Mitteilungen, Zeitschrift des Wirtschafts- und Sozialwissenschaftlichen Instituts des Deutschen Gewerkschaftsbundes, 34, 4, 194-203.

Bahrdt, Hans Paul (1984). Muhe und Arbeit. Zum Wandel der Einstellung zur Arbeit in der Geschichte. In: Kerber, W. (Hg.): Arbeitswelt im Umbruch. Arbeitslosigkeit als Anstoss und Herausforderung, Dusseldorf.

Beck-Gernsheim, Elisabeth (1980). Das halbierte Leben. Mannerwelt Beruf, Frauenwelt Familie, Frankfurt.

Behrens, Johann (1982). Die Ausdifferenzierung der Arbeit. In Hondrich, Karl Otto (Hg.): Soziale Differenzierung, Langzeitanalysen zum Wandel von Politik, Arbeit und Familie, Frankfurt/New York.

Benseler, F., Heinze, R.G. and Klonne, A. (Hg.) (1982). Zukunft der Arbeit. Eigenarbeit, Alternativokonomie?., Hamburg.

Berger, Johannes (1983). Die Wiederkehr der Vollbeschaftigungslucke, Entwicklungslinien des wohlfaahrtsstaatlichen Kapitalismus. In: Matthes, Joachim (Hg.): Krise der Arbeitsgesellschaft? Verhandlungen des 21. Deutschen Soziologentages in Bamberg 1982, Frankfurt/New York.

Born, Claudia and Vollmer, Christine (1983). Familienfreundliche Gestaltung des Arbeitslebens. Schriftenreihe des Bundesministers fur Jugend, Familie und Gesundheit, Band 135, Stuttgart/Berlin/Koln/Mainz.

Burgdorff, Stephan and Meyer-Larsen, Werner (Hg.) (1984). Weniger Arbeit. Die Uberlebenschancen der Industriegesellschaft. Spiegel-Buch, Hamburg.

Conradi, H. (1982). Teilzeitarbeit. Theorie, Realitat, Realisierbarkeit. Beitrage zur Sozialokonomik der Arbeit, Band 5, Munchen.

Dahrendorf, Ralf (1983). Wenn der Arbeitsgesellschaft die Arbeit ausgeht. In: Matthes, Joachim

# Bibliography

(Hg.): Krise der Arbeitsgesellschaft? Verhandlungen des 21. Deutschen Soziologentages im
Bamberg 1982. Frankfurt/New York.

Eckart, Ch. (1984). Die Teilzeitarbeit von Frauen.
Eine prekare Strategie gegen Einseitigkeit und
Doppelbelastung. In: Feministische Studien,
1984, 19-31.

Erler, G.A. (1985). Frauenzimmer. Fur eine Politik
des Unterschieds, Berlin.

Erler, G., Jaeckel, M. and Sass, J. (1983). Mutter
zwischen Beruf und Familie. Familienpolitik mit
Mutterschaftsurlaub, Elternurlaub oder
Erziehungsgeld? Modelle und Meinungen aus funf
europaischen Landern, Munchen.

Gerzer, A.,Jaeckel, M. and Sass, J. (1985). Flexible
Arbeitszeit - vor allem ein Frauenthema. Die
Beispiele Ikea und Kaufhaus Beck. In: Das Ende
der starren Arbeitszeit, hrsg. von Thomas
Schmid, Berlin, 97 - 127.

Inglehart, Ronald (1979). Wertwandel in den west-
lichen Gesellschaften, Politische Konsequenzen
von materialistischen und postmaterialistischen
Prioritaten. In: Klages, H. and Kmieciak, P.
(Hg.): Wertwandel und gesellschaftlicher Wandel,
Frankfurt.

Matthes, J. (Hg.) (1983). Krise der Arbeitsgesellschaft? Verhandlungen des 21. Deutschen
Soziologentages in Bamberg, Frankfurt/New York.

Mayr, H. and Janssen, H. (Hg.) (1984). Perspek-
tiven der Arbeitszeitverkurzung, Wissenschaft-
ler und Gewerkschaftler zur 35-Stunden-Woche.
Beitrage zur wissenschaftlichen Arbeitstagung
der IG Metall fur die Bundesrepublik Deutsch-
land vom 24. bis 26. April 1983, Koln.

Muller, W., Willms, A. and Handl, J. (Hg.) (1983).
Strukturwandel der Frauenarbeit 1880-1980,
Frankfurt/New York.

Noelle-Neumann, E. and Strumpel, B. (1984). Macht
Arbeit krank? Macht Arbeit glucklich? Eine
aktuelle Kontroverse. Munchen/Zurich.

Offe, C., Hindrichs, K. and Wiesenthal, H. (Hg.)
(1982). Arbeitspolitik. Formen und Folgen einer
Neuverteilung der Arbeitszeit. Frankfurt/New
York.

Ostner, Illona (1970). Beruf und Hausarbeit.
Frankfurt.

Ostner, Illona and Willms, Angelika (1983). Struk-
tuelle Veranderungen der Frauenarbeit in Haus-
halt und Beruf. In: Matthes, Joachim (Hg.):
Krise der Arbeitsgesellschaft? Verhandlungen
des 21. Deutschen Soziologentages in Bamberg

Bibliography

1982. Frankfurt/New York.
Pape-Siebert, S. (1984). Genug gejammert - oder
    verraten die Frauen den Feminismus? Eine
    Streitschrift. Berlin.
Peters, A. (1984). Frauenerwerbstatigkeit.
    Literaturdokumentation des Instituts fur Ar-
    beitsmarkt- und Berufsforschung der Bundesan-
    stalt fur Arbeit. Nurnberg.
Rudolph, H., Duran, M., Klahn, M., Nassauer, M. and
Naumann, J. Chancen und Risiken neuer Arbeitszeit-
    systeme. Zur Situation teilseitarbeitender
    Frauen im Berliner Einzelhandel. In: WSI-Mit-
    teilungen, Zeitschrift des Wirtschafts- und
    Sozialwissenschaftlichen Instituts des
    Deutschen Gewerkschaftbundes, 34 (1981) 4, 194-
    203.
Wiesenthal, H., Offe, C., Hinrichs, K. and Engfer,
    U. Arbeitsszeitflexibilisierung und gewerk-
    schaftliche Interessenvertretung. Regelungs-
    probleme und Risiken individueller Arbeitszei-
    ten. In: WSI-Mitteilungen, Zeitschrift des
    Wirtschafts- und Sozialwissenschaftlichen
    Instituts des Deutschen Gewerkschaftbundes,
    10/1983, 585-595.

For Product Safety Concerns and Information please contact our EU
representative GPSR@taylorandfrancis.com
Taylor & Francis Verlag GmbH, Kaufingerstraße 24, 80331 München, Germany